The Barbarism of Berlin

and

Utopia of Usurers and Other Essays

by

G.K. Chesterton

NATAL PUBLISHING LLC
ARS LONGA, VITA BREVIS

Copyright© 2024 Natal Publishing

All rights reserved

Cover art by Mauricio A. on Pixabay

CONTENTS

INTRODUCTION: THE FACTS OF THE CASE

Unless we are all mad, there is at the back of the most bewildering business a story: and if we are all mad, there is no such thing as madness. If I set a house on fire, it is quite true that I may illuminate many other people's weaknesses as well as my own. It may be that the master of the house was burned because he was drunk: it may be that the mistress of the house was burned because she was stingy, and perished arguing about the expense of a fire-escape. It is, nevertheless, broadly true that they both were burned because I set fire to their house. That is the story of the thing. The mere facts of the story about the present European conflagration are quite as easy to tell.

Before we go on to the deeper things which make this war the most sincere war of human history, it is as easy to answer the question of why England came to be in it at all, as it is to ask how a man fell down a coal-hole, or failed to keep an appointment. Facts are not the whole truth. But facts are facts, and in this case the facts are few and simple. Prussia, France, and England had all promised not to invade Belgium. Prussia proposed to invade Belgium, because it was the safest way of invading France. But Prussia promised that if she might break in, through her own broken promise and ours, she would break in and not steal. In other words, we were offered at the same instant a promise of faith in the future and a proposal of perjury in the present. Those interested in human origins may refer to an old Victorian writer of English, who, in the last and most restrained of his historical essays, wrote of Frederick the Great, the founder of this unchanging Prussian policy. After describing how Frederick broke the guarantee he had signed on behalf of Maria Theresa, he then describes how Frederick sought to put things straight by a promise that was an insult. "If she would but let him have Silesia, he would, he said, stand by her against any power which should try to deprive her of her other dominions, as if he was not already bound to stand by her, or as if his new promise could be of more value than the old one." That passage was written by Macaulay, but so far as the mere contemporary facts are concerned it might have been written by me.

Upon the immediate logical and legal origin of the English interest there can be no rational debate. There are some things so simple that one can almost prove them with plans and diagrams, as in Euclid. One could make a kind of comic calendar of what would have happened to the English diplomatist, if he had been silenced every time by Prussian diplomacy. Suppose we arrange it in the form of a kind of diary:

July 24: Germany invades Belgium.
July 25: England declares war.
July 26: Germany promises not to annex Belgium.
July 27: England withdraws from the war.
July 28: Germany annexes Belgium, England declares war.
July 29: Germany promises not to annex France, England withdraws from the war.
July 30: Germany annexes France, England declares war.
July 31: Germany promises not to annex England.
Aug. 1: England withdraws from the war. Germany invades England.

How long is anybody expected to go on with that sort of game; or keep peace at that illimitable price? How long must we pursue a road in which promises are all fetishes in front of us; and all fragments behind us? No; upon the cold facts of the final negotiations, as told by any of the diplomatists in any of the documents, there is no doubt about the story. And no doubt about the villain of the story.

These are the last facts; the facts which involved England. It is equally easy to state the first facts; the facts which involved Europe. The prince who practically ruled Austria was shot by certain persons whom the Austrian Government believed to be conspirators from Servia. The Austrian Government piled up arms and armies, but said not a word either to Servia their suspect, or Italy their ally. From the documents it would seem that Austria kept everybody in the dark, except Prussia. It is probably nearer the truth to say that Prussia kept everybody in the dark, including Austria. But all that is what is called opinion, belief, conviction, or common sense: and we are not dealing with it here. The objective fact is that Austria told Servia to permit Servian officers to be suspended by the authority of

Austrian officers; and told Servia to submit to this within forty-eight hours. In other words, the Sovereign of Servia was practically told to take off not only the laurels of two great campaigns, but his own lawful and national crown, and to do it in a time in which no respectable citizen is expected to discharge an hotel bill. Servia asked for time for arbitration—in short, for peace. But Russia had already begun to mobilise; and Prussia, presuming that Servia might thus be rescued, declared war.

Between these two ends of fact, the ultimatum to Servia, the ultimatum to Belgium, anyone so inclined can of course talk as if everything were relative. If anyone asks why the Czar should rush to the support of Servia, it is easy to ask why the Kaiser should rush to the support of Austria. If anyone says that the French would attack the Germans, it is sufficient to answer that the Germans did attack the French. There remain, however, two attitudes to consider, even perhaps two arguments to counter, which can best be considered and countered under this general head of facts. First of all, there is a curious, cloudy sort of argument, much affected by the professional rhetoricians of Prussia, who are sent out to instruct and correct the minds of Americans or Scandinavians. It consists of going into convulsions of incredulity and scorn at the mention of Russia's responsibility of Servia, or England's responsibility of Belgium; and suggesting that, treaty or no treaty, frontier or no frontier, Russia would be out to slay Teutons or England to steal Colonies. Here, as elsewhere, I think the professors dotted all over the Baltic plain fail in lucidity and in the power of distinguishing ideas. Of course it is quite true that England has material interests to defend, and will probably use the opportunity to defend them; or, in other words, of course England, like everybody else, would be more comfortable if Prussia were less predominant.

The fact remains that we did not do what the Germans did. We did not invade Holland to seize a naval and commercial advantage; and whether they say that we wished to do it in our greed, or feared to do it in our cowardice, the fact remains that we did not do it. Unless this commonsense principle be kept in view, I cannot conceive how any quarrel can possibly be judged. A contract may be made between two persons solely for material advantage on each side: but the moral advantage is still generally supposed to lie with the person who keeps the contract. Surely it cannot be dishonest to be honest—even if honesty is the best policy. Imagine the most complex maze of indirect motive; and still the man who keeps faith for money cannot possibly be worse than the man who breaks faith for money. It will be noted that this ultimate test applies in the same way to Servia as to Belgium and Britain. The Servians may not be a very peaceful people, but on the occasion under discussion it was certainly they who wanted peace. You may choose to think the Serb a sort of born robber: but on this occasion it was certainly the Austrian who was trying to rob. Similarly, you may call England perfidious as a sort of historical summary; and declare your private belief that Mr. Asquith was vowed from infancy to the ruin of the German Empire, a Hannibal and hater of the eagles. But, when all is said, it is nonsense to call a man perfidious because he keeps his promise. It is absurd to complain of the sudden treachery of a business man in turning up punctually to his appointment: or the unfair shock given to a creditor by the debtor paying his debts.

Lastly, there is an attitude, not unknown in the crisis, against which I should particularly like to protest. I should address my protest especially to those lovers and pursuers of peace who, very shortsightedly, have occasionally adopted it. I mean the attitude which is impatient of these preliminary details about who did this or that, and whether it was right or wrong. They are satisfied with saying that an enormous calamity, called war, has been begun by some or all of us and should be ended by some or all of us. To these people, this preliminary chapter about the precise happenings must appear not only dry (and it must of necessity be the driest part of the task) but essentially needless and barren. I wish to tell these people that they are wrong; that they are wrong upon all principles of human justice and historic continuity; but that they are specially and supremely wrong upon their own principles of arbitration and international peace.

These sincere and high-minded peace-lovers are always telling us that citizens no longer settle their quarrels by private violence; and that nations should no longer settle theirs by public violence. They are always telling us that we no longer fight duels; and need not wage wars. In short, they perpetually base their peace proposals on the fact that an ordinary citizen no longer avenges himself with an axe. But how is he prevented from revenging himself with an axe? If he hits his neighbour on the head with the kitchen chopper, what do we do? Do we all join hands, like children playing Mulberry Bush, and say, "We are all responsible for this; but let us hope it will not spread. Let us hope for the happy day when we shall leave off chopping at the man's head; and when nobody shall ever chop anything for ever and ever." Do we say, "Let bygones be bygones; why go back to all the dull details with which the business began; who can tell with what sinister motives the man was standing there, within reach of the hatchet?" We do not. We keep the peace in private life by asking for the facts of provocation, and the proper object of punishment. We do go into the dull details; we do enquire into the origins; we do emphatically enquire who it was that hit first. In short, we do what I have done very briefly in this place.

Given this, it is indeed true that behind these facts there are truths; truths of a terrible, of a spiritual sort. In mere fact, the Germanic power has been wrong about Servia, wrong about Russia, wrong about Belgium, wrong about England, wrong about Italy. But there was a reason for its being wrong everywhere; and of that root reason, which has moved half the world against it, I shall speak later in this series. For that is something too omnipresent to be proved, too indisputable to be helped by detail. It is nothing less than the locating, after more than a hundred years of recriminations and wrong explanations, of the modern European evil; the finding of the fountain from which poison has flowed upon all the nations of the earth.

I. THE WAR ON THE WORD

It will hardly be denied that there is one lingering doubt in many, who recognise unavoidable self-defence in the instant parry of the English sword, and who have no great love for the sweeping sabre of Sadowa and Sedan. That doubt is the doubt whether Russia, as compared with Prussia, is sufficiently decent and democratic to be the ally of liberal and civilised powers. I take first, therefore, this matter of civilisation.

It is vital in a discussion like this that we should make sure we are going by meanings and not by mere words. It is not necessary in any argument to settle what a word means or ought to mean. But it is necessary in every argument to settle what we propose to mean by the word. So long as our opponent understands what is the *thing* of which we are talking, it does not matter to the argument whether the word is or is not the one he would have chosen. A soldier does not say "We were ordered to go to Mechlin; but I would rather go to Malines." He may discuss the etymology and archaeology of the difference on the march: but the point is that he knows where to go. So long as we know what a given word is to mean in a given discussion, it does not even matter if it means something else in some other and quite distinct discussion. We have a perfect right to say that the width of a window comes to four feet; even if we instantly and cheerfully change the subject to the larger mammals, and say that an elephant has four feet. The identity of the words does not matter, because there is no doubt at all about the meanings; because nobody is likely to think of an elephant as four feet long, or of a window as having tusks and a curly trunk.

It is essential to emphasise this consciousness of the *thing* under discussion in connection with two or three words that are, as it were, the key-words of this war. One of them is the word "barbarian." The Prussians apply it to the Russians: the Russians apply it to the Prussians. Both, I think, really mean something that really exists, name or no name. Both mean different things. And if we ask what these different things are, we shall understand why England and France prefer Russia; and consider Prussia the really dangerous barbarian of the two. To begin with, it goes so much deeper even than atrocities; of which, in the past at least, all the three Empires of Central

Europe have partaken pretty equally, as they partook of Poland. An English writer, seeking to avert the war by warnings against Russian influence, said that the flogged backs of Polish women stood between us and the Alliance. But not long before, the flogging of women by an Austrian general led to that officer being thrashed in the streets of London by Barclay and Perkins' draymen. And as for the third power, the Prussians, it seems clear that they have treated Belgian women in a style compared with which flogging might be called an official formality. But, as I say, something much deeper than any such recrimination lies behind the use of the word on either side. When the German Emperor complains of our allying ourselves with a barbaric and half-oriental power, he is not (I assure you) shedding tears over the grave of Kosciusko. And when I say (as I do most heartily) that the German Emperor is a barbarian, I am not merely expressing any prejudices I may have against the profanation of churches or of children. My countrymen and I mean a certain and intelligible thing when we call the Prussians barbarians. It is quite different from the thing attributed to Russians; and it could not possibly be attributed to Russians. It is very important that the neutral world should understand what this thing is.

If the German calls the Russian barbarous, he presumably means imperfectly civilised. There is a certain path along which Western nations have proceeded in recent times, and it is tenable that Russia has not proceeded so far as the others: that she has less of the special modern system in science, commerce, machinery, travel, or political constitution. The Russ ploughs with an old plough; he wears a wild beard; he adores relics; his life is as rude and hard as that of a subject of Alfred the Great. Therefore he is, in the German sense, a barbarian. Poor fellows like Gorky and Dostoieffsky have to form their own reflections on the scenery without the assistance of large quotations from Schiller on garden seats, or inscriptions directing them to pause and thank the All-Father for the finest view in Hesse-Pumpernickel. The Russians, having nothing but their faith, their fields, their great courage, and their self-governing communes, are quite cut off from what is called (in the fashionable street in Frankfort) The True, The Beautiful and The Good. There is a real sense in which one can call such backwardness barbaric, by comparison with the Kaiserstrasse;

and in that sense it is true of Russia.

Now we, the French and English, do not mean this when we call the Prussians barbarians. If their cities soared higher than their flying ships, if their trains travelled faster than their bullets, we should still call them barbarians. We should know exactly what we meant by it; and we should know that it is true. For we do not mean anything that is an imperfect civilisation by accident. We mean something that is the enemy of civilisation by design. We mean something that is wilfully at war with the principles by which human society has been made possible hitherto. Of course it must be partly civilised even to destroy civilisation. Such ruin could not be wrought by the savages that are merely undeveloped or inert. You could not have even Huns without horses; or horses without horsemanship. You could not have even Danish pirates without ships, or ships without seamanship. This person, whom I may call the Positive Barbarian, must be rather more superficially up-to-date than what I may call the Negative Barbarian. Alaric was an officer in the Roman legions: but for all that he destroyed Rome. Nobody supposes that Eskimos could have done it at all neatly. But (in our meaning) barbarism is not a matter of methods, but of aims. We say that these veneered vandals have the perfectly serious aim of destroying certain ideas, which, as they think, the world has outgrown; without which, as we think, the world will die.

It is essential that this perilous peculiarity in the Pruss, or Positive Barbarian, should be seized. He has what he fancies is a new idea; and he is going to apply it to everybody. As a fact it is simply a false generalisation; but he is really trying to make it general. This does not apply to the Negative Barbarian: it does not apply to the Russian or the Servian, even if they are barbarians. If a Russian peasant does beat his wife, he does it because his fathers did it before him: he is likely to beat less rather than more, as the past fades away. He does not think, as the Prussian would, that he has made a new discovery in physiology in finding that a woman is weaker than a man. If a Servian does knife his rival without a word, he does it because other Servians have done it. He may regard it even as piety, but certainly not as progress. He does not think, as the Prussian does, that he founds a new school of horology by starting before the word "Go." He does not think he is in advance of the world in militarism merely because he is behind it in morals. No; the danger of the Pruss is that he is prepared to fight for old errors as if they were new truths. He has somehow heard of certain shallow simplifications, and imagines that we have never heard of them. And, as I have said, his limited, but very sincere lunacy concentrates chiefly in a desire to destroy two ideas, the twin root ideas of rational society. The first is the idea of record and promise: the second is the idea of reciprocity.

It is plain that the promise, or extension of responsibility through time, is what chiefly distinguishes us, I will not say from savages, but from brutes and reptiles. This was noted by the shrewdness of the Old Testament, when it summed up the dark irresponsible enormity of Leviathan in the words, "Will he make a pact with thee?" The promise, like the wheel, is unknown in Nature: and is the first mark of man. Referring only to human civilisation, it may be said with seriousness that in the beginning was the Word. The vow is to the man what the song is to the bird, or the bark to the dog; his voice, whereby he is known. Just as a man who cannot keep an appointment is not fit even to fight a duel, so the man who cannot keep an appointment with himself is not sane enough even for suicide. It is not easy to mention anything on which the enormous apparatus of human life can be said to depend. But if it depends on anything, it is on this frail cord, flung from the forgotten hills of yesterday to the invisible mountains of to-morrow. On that solitary string hangs everything from Armageddon to an almanac, from a successful revolution to a return ticket. On that solitary string the Barbarian is hacking heavily, with a sabre which is fortunately blunt.

Anyone can see this well enough, merely by reading the last negotiations between London and Berlin. The Prussians had made a new discovery in international politics: that it may often be convenient to make a promise; and yet curiously inconvenient to keep it. They were charmed, in their simple way, with this scientific discovery, and desired to communicate it to the world. They therefore promised England a promise, on condition that she broke a promise, and on the implied condition that the new promise might be broken as easily as the old one. To the profound astonishment of Prussia, this reasonable offer was refused! I believe that the astonishment of Prussia was quite sincere. That is what I mean when I say that the Barbarian is trying to cut away that cord of honesty and clear record on which hangs all that men have made.

The friends of the German cause have complained that Asiatics and Africans upon the very verge of savagery have been brought against them from India and Algiers. And in ordinary circumstances, I should sympathise with such a complaint made by a European people. But the circumstances are not ordinary. Here, again, the quiet unique barbarism of Prussia goes deeper than what we call barbarities. About mere barbarities, it is true, the Turco and the Sikh would have a very good reply to the superior Teuton. The general and just reason for not using non-European tribes against Europeans is that given by Chatham against the use of the Red Indian: that such allies might do very diabolical things. But the poor Turco might not unreasonably ask, after a week-end in Belgium, what more diabolical things he *could* do than the highly cultured Germans were doing themselves. Nevertheless, as I say, the justification of any extra-European aid goes deeper than any such details. It rests upon the fact that even other civilisations, even much lower civilisations, even remote and repulsive civilisations, depend as much as our own on this primary principle, on which the super-morality of Potsdam declares open War. Even savages promise things; and respect those who keep their promises. Even Orientals write things down: and though they write them from right to left, they know the importance of a scrap of paper. Many merchants will tell you that the word of the sinister and almost unhuman Chinaman is often as good as his bond: and it was amid palm trees and Syrian pavilions that the great utterance opened the tabernacle to him that sweareth to his hurt and changeth not. There is doubtless a dense labyrinth of duplicity in the East, and perhaps more guile in the individual Asiatic than in the individual German. But we are not talking of the violations of human morality in various parts of the world. We are talking about a new and inhuman morality, which denies altogether the day of obligation. The Prussians have been told by their literary men that everything depends upon Mood: and by their politicians that all arrangements dissolve before "necessity." That is the importance of the

German Chancellor's phrase. He did not allege some special excuse in the case of Belgium, which might make it seem an exception that proved the rule. He distinctly argued, as on a principle applicable to other cases, that victory was a necessity and honour was a scrap of paper. And it is evident that the half-educated Prussian imagination really cannot get any farther than this. It cannot see that if everybody's action were entirely incalculable from hour to hour, it would not only be the end of all promises, but the end of all projects. In not being able to see that, the Berlin philosopher is really on a lower mental level than the Arab who respects the salt, or the Brahmin who preserves the caste. And in this quarrel we have a right to come with scimitars as well as sabres, with bows as well as rifles, with assegai and tomahawk and boomerang, because there is in all these at least a seed of civilisation that these intellectual anarchists would kill. And if they should find us in our last stand girt with such strange swords and following unfamiliar ensigns, and ask us for what we fight in so singular a company, we shall know what to reply: "We fight for the trust and for the tryst; for fixed memories and the possible meeting of men; for all that makes life anything but an uncontrollable nightmare. We fight for the long arm of honour and remembrance; for all that can lift a man above the quicksands of his moods, and give him the mastery of time."

II. THE REFUSAL OF RECIPROCITY

In the last summary I suggested that Barbarism, as we mean it, is not mere ignorance or even mere cruelty. It has a more precise sense, and means militant hostility to certain necessary human ideas. I took the case of the vow or the contract, which Prussian intellectualism would destroy. I urged that the Prussian is a spiritual Barbarian, because he is not bound by his own past, any more than a man in a dream. He avows that when he promised to respect a frontier on Monday, he did not foresee what he calls "the necessity" of not respecting it on Tuesday. In short, he is like a child, who at the end of all reasonable explanations and reminders of admitted arrangements has no answer except "But I *want* to."

There is another idea in human arrangements so fundamental as to be forgotten; but now for the first time denied. It may be called the idea of reciprocity; or, in better English, of give and take. The Prussian appears to be quite intellectually incapable of this thought. He cannot, I think, conceive the idea that is the foundation of all comedy; that, in the eyes of the other man, he is only the other man. And if we carry this clue through the institutions of Prussianised Germany, we shall find how curiously his mind has been limited in the matter. The German differs from other patriots in the inability to understand patriotism. Other European peoples pity the Poles or the Welsh for their violated borders; but Germans only pity themselves. They might take forcible possession of the Severn or the Danube, of the Thames or the Tiber, of the Garry or the Garonne—and they would still be singing sadly about how fast and true stands the watch on Rhine; and what a shame it would be if anyone took their own little river away from them. That is what I mean by not being reciprocal: and you will find it in all that they do: as in all that is done by savages.

Here, again, it is very necessary to avoid confusing this soul of the savage with mere savagery in the sense of brutality or butchery; in which the Greeks, the French and all the most civilised nations have indulged in hours of abnormal panic or revenge. Accusations of cruelty are generally mutual. But it is the point about the Prussian that with him nothing is mutual. The definition of the true savage does not concern itself even with how much more he hurts strangers or captives than do the other tribes of men. The definition of the true savage is that he laughs when he hurts you; and howls when you hurt him. This extraordinary inequality in the mind is in every act and word that comes from Berlin. For instance, no man of the world believes all he sees in the newspapers; and no journalist believes a quarter of it. We should, therefore, be quite ready in the ordinary way to take a great deal off the tales of German atrocities; to doubt this story or deny that. But there is one thing that we cannot doubt or deny: the seal and authority of the Emperor. In the Imperial proclamation the fact that certain "frightful" things have been done is admitted; and justified on the ground of their frightfulness. It was a military necessity to terrify the peaceful populations with something that was not civilised, something that was hardly human. Very well. That is an intelligible policy: and in that sense an intelligible argument. An army endangered by foreigners may do the most frightful things. But then we turn the next page of the Kaiser's public diary, and we find him writing to the President of the United States, to complain that the English are using dum-dum bullets and violating various regulations of the Hague Conference. I pass for the present the question of whether there is a word of truth in these charges. I am content to gaze rapturously at the blinking eyes of the True, or Positive, Barbarian. I suppose he would be quite puzzled if we said that violating the Hague Conference was "a military necessity" to us; or that the rules of the Conference were only a scrap of paper. He would be quite pained if we said that dum-dum bullets, "by their very frightfulness," would be very useful to keep conquered Germans in order. Do what he will, he cannot get outside the idea that he, because he is he and not you, is free to break the law; and also to appeal to the law. It is said that the Prussian officers play at a game called Kriegsspiel, or the War Game. But in truth they could not play at any game; for the essence of every game is that the rules are the same on both sides.

But taking every German institution in turn, the case is the same; and it is not a case of mere bloodshed or military bravado. The duel, for example, can legitimately be called a barbaric thing; but the word is here used in another sense. There are duels in Germany; but so there are in France, Italy, Belgium and

Spain; indeed, there are duels wherever there are dentists, newspapers, Turkish baths, time-tables, and all the curses of civilisation; except in England and a corner of America. You may happen to regard the duel as an historic relic of the more barbaric States on which these modern States were built. It might equally well be maintained that the duel is everywhere the sign of high civilisation; being the sign of its more delicate sense of honour, its more vulnerable vanity, or its greater dread of social disrepute. But whichever of the two views you take, you must concede that the essence of the duel is an armed equality. I should not, therefore, apply the word barbaric, as I am using it, to the duels of German officers or even to the broadsword combats that are conventional among the German students. I do not see why a young Prussian should not have scars all over his face if he likes them; nay, they are often the redeeming points of interest on an otherwise somewhat unenlightening countenance. The duel may be defended; the sham duel may be defended.

What cannot be defended is something really peculiar to Prussia, of which we hear numberless stories, some of them certainly true. It might be called the one-sided duel. I mean the idea that there is some sort of dignity in drawing the sword upon a man who has not got a sword; a waiter, or a shop assistant, or even a schoolboy. One of the officers of the Kaiser in the affair at Saberne was found industriously hacking at a cripple. In all these matters I would avoid sentiment. We must not lose our tempers at the mere cruelty of the thing; but pursue the strict psychological distinction. Others besides German soldiers have slain the defenceless, for loot or lust or private malice, like any other murderer. The point is that nowhere else but in Prussian Germany is any theory of honour mixed up with such things; any more than with poisoning or picking pockets. No French, English, Italian or American gentleman would think he had in some way cleared his own character by sticking his sabre through some ridiculous greengrocer who had nothing in his hand but a cucumber. It would seem as if the word which is translated from the German as "honour," must really mean something quite different in German. It seems to mean something more like what we should call "prestige."

The fundamental fact, however, is the absence of the

reciprocal idea. The Prussian is not sufficiently civilised for the duel. Even when he crosses swords with us his thoughts are not as our thoughts; when we both glorify war, we are glorifying different things. Our medals are wrought like his, but they do not mean the same thing; our regiments are cheered as his are, but the thought in the heart is not the same; the Iron Cross is on the bosom of his king, but it is not the sign of our God. For we, alas, follow our God with many relapses and self-contradictions, but he follows his very consistently. Through all the things that we have examined, the view of national boundaries, the view of military methods, the view of personal honour and self-defence, there runs in their case something of an atrocious simplicity; something too simple for us to understand: the idea that glory consists in holding the steel, and not in facing it.

If further examples were necessary, it would be easy to give hundreds of them. Let us leave, for the moment, the relation between man and man in the thing called the duel. Let us take the relation between man and woman, in that immortal duel which we call a marriage. Here again we shall find that other Christian civilisations aim at some kind of equality; even if the balance be irrational or dangerous. Thus, the two extremes of the treatment of women might be represented by what are called the respectable classes in America and in France. In America they choose the risk of comradeship; in France the compensation of courtesy. In America it is practically possible for any young gentleman to take any young lady for what he calls (I deeply regret to say) a joyride; but at least the man goes with the woman as much as the woman with the man. In France the young woman is protected like a nun while she is unmarried; but when she is a mother she is really a holy woman; and when she is a grandmother she is a holy terror. By both extremes the woman gets something back out of life. There is only one place where she gets little or nothing back; and that is the north of Germany. France and America aim alike at equality—America by similarity; France by dissimilarity. But North Germany does definitely aim at inequality. The woman stands up, with no more irritation than a butler; the man sits down, with no more embarrassment than a guest. This is the cool affirmation of inferiority, as in the case of the sabre and the tradesman. "Thou goest with women; forget not thy whip," said Nietzsche. It will be observed that he does not say "poker"; which might come more naturally to the mind of a more common or Christian wife-beater. But then a poker is a part of domesticity; and might be used by the wife as well as the husband. In fact, it often, is. The sword and the whip are the weapons of a privileged caste.

Pass from the closest of all differences, that between husband and wife, to the most distant of all differences, that of the remote and unrelated races who have seldom seen each other's faces, and never been tinged with each other's blood. Here we still find the same unvarying Prussian principle. Any European might feel a genuine fear of the Yellow Peril; and many Englishmen, Frenchmen, and Russians have felt and expressed it. Many might say, and have said, that the Heathen Chinee is very heathen indeed; that if he ever advances against us he will trample and torture and utterly destroy, in a way that Eastern people do, but Western people do not. Nor do I doubt the German Emperor's sincerity when he sought to point out to us how abnormal and abominable such a nightmare campaign would be, supposing that it could ever come. But now comes the comic irony; which never fails to follow on the attempt of the Prussian to be philosophic. For the Kaiser, after explaining to his troops how important it was to avoid Eastern Barbarism, instantly commanded them to become Eastern Barbarians. He told them, in so many words, to be Huns: and leave nothing living or standing behind them. In fact, he frankly offered a new army corps of aboriginal Tartars to the Far East, within such time as it may take a bewildered Hanoverian to turn into a Tartar. Anyone who has the painful habit of personal thought will perceive here at once the non-reciprocal principle again. Boiled down to its bones of logic, it means simply this: "I am a German and you are a Chinaman. Therefore I, being a German, have a right to be a Chinaman. But you have no right to be a Chinaman; because you are only a Chinaman." This is probably the highest point to which German culture has risen.

The principle here neglected, which may be called Mutuality by those who misunderstand and dislike the word Equality, does not offer so clear a distinction between the Prussian and the other peoples as did the first Prussian principle of an infinite and destructive opportunism; or, in other words, the principle of being unprincipled. Nor upon this second can one take up so obvious a position touching the other civilisations or semi-civilisations of the world. Some idea of oath and bond there is in the rudest tribes, in the darkest continents. But it might be maintained, of the more delicate and imaginative element of reciprocity, that a cannibal in Borneo understands it almost as little as a professor in Berlin. A narrow and one-sided seriousness is the fault of barbarians all over the world. This may have been the meaning, for aught I know, of the one eye of the Cyclops: that the Barbarian cannot see round things or look at them from two points of view; and thus becomes a blind beast and an eater of men. Certainly there can be no better summary of the savage than this, which, as we have seen, unfits him for the duel. He is the man who cannot love—no, nor even hate—his neighbour as himself.

But this quality in Prussia does have one effect which has reference to the same quest of the lower civilisations. It disposes once and for all at least of the civilising mission of Germany. Evidently the Germans are the last people in the world to be trusted with the task. They are as shortsighted morally as physically. What is their sophism of "necessity" but an inability to imagine to-morrow morning? What is their non-reciprocity but an inability to imagine, not a god or devil, but merely another man? Are these to judge mankind? Men of two tribes in Africa not only know that they are all men, but can understand that they are all black men. In this they are quite seriously in advance of the intellectual Prussian; who cannot be got to see that we are all white men. The ordinary eye is unable to perceive in the North-East Teuton, anything that marks him out especially from the more colourless classes of the rest of Aryan mankind. He is simply a white man, with a tendency to the grey or the drab. Yet he will explain, in serious official documents, that the difference between him and us is a difference between "the master-race and the inferior-race." The collapse of German philosophy always occurs at the beginning, rather than the end of an argument; and the difficulty here is that there is no way of testing which is a master-race except by asking which is your own race. If you cannot find out (as is usually the case) you fall back on the absurd occupation of writing history about prehistoric times. But I suggest quite seriously that if the Germans can give their philosophy to the Hottentots, there is no reason why they should not give their sense of superiority to the Hottentots. If they can see such fine shades between the Goth and the Gaul, there is no reason why similar shades should not lift the savage above other savages; why any Ojibway should not discover that he is one tint redder than the Dacotahs; or any nigger in the Cameroons say he is not so black as he is painted. For this principle of a quite unproved racial supremacy is the last and worst of the refusals of reciprocity. The Prussian calls all men to admire the beauty of his large blue eyes. If they do, it is because they have inferior eyes: if they don't, it is because they have no eyes.

Wherever the most miserable remnant of our race, astray and dried up in deserts, or buried for ever under the fall of bad civilisations, has some feeble memory that men are men, that bargains are bargains, that there are two sides to a question, or even that it takes two to make a quarrel—that remnant has the right to resist the New Culture, to the knife and club and the splintered stone. For the Prussian begins all his culture by that act which is the destruction of all creative thought and constructive action. He breaks that mirror in the mind, in which a man can see the face of his friend and foe.

III. THE APPETITE OF TYRANNY

The German Emperor has reproached this country with allying itself with "barbaric and semi-oriental power." We have already considered in what sense we use the word barbaric: it is in the sense of one who is hostile to civilisation, not one who is insufficient in it. But when we pass from the idea of the barbaric to the idea of the oriental, the case is even more curious. There is nothing particularly Tartar in Russian affairs, except the fact that Russia expelled the Tartars. The eastern invader occupied and crushed the country for many years; but that is equally true of Greece, of Spain, and even of Austria. If Russia has suffered from the East she has suffered in order to resist it: and it is rather hard that the very miracle of her escape should make a mystery about her origin. Jonah may or may not have been three days inside a fish, but that does not make him a merman. And in all the other cases of European nations who escaped the monstrous captivity, we do admit the purity and continuity of the European type. We consider the old Eastern rule as a wound, but not as a stain. Copper-coloured men out of Africa overruled for centuries the religion and patriotism of Spaniards. Yet I have never heard that Don Quixote was an African fable on the lines of Uncle Remus. I have never heard that the heavy black in the pictures of Velasquez was due to a negro ancestry. In the case of Spain, which is close to us, we can recognise the resurrection of a Christian and cultured nation after its age of bondage. But Russia is rather remote; and those to whom nations are but names in newspapers can really fancy, like Mr. Baring's friend, that all Russian churches are "mosques." Yet the land of Turgeniev is not a wilderness of fakirs; and even the fanatical Russian is as proud of being different from the Mongol, as the fanatical Spaniard was proud of being different from the Moor.

The town of Reading, as it exists, offers few opportunities for piracy on the high seas: yet it was the camp of the pirates in Alfred's day. I should think it hard to call the people of Berkshire half-Danish, merely because they drove out the Danes. In short, some temporary submergence under the savage flood was the fate of many of the most civilised states of Christendom; and it is quite ridiculous to argue that Russia, which wrestled hardest, must have recovered least.

Everywhere, doubtless, the East spread a sort of enamel over the conquered countries, but everywhere the enamel cracked. Actual history, in fact, is exactly opposite to the cheap proverb invented against the Muscovite. It is not true to say "Scratch a Russian and you find a Tartar." In the darkest hour of the barbaric dominion it was truer to say, "Scratch a Tartar and you find a Russian." It was the civilisation that survived under all the barbarism. This vital romance of Russia, this revolution against Asia, can be proved in pure fact; not only from the almost superhuman activity of Russia during the struggle, but also (which is much rarer as human history goes) by her quite consistent conduct since. She is the only great nation which has really expelled the Mongol from her country, and continued to protest against the presence of the Mongol in her continent. Knowing what he had been in Russia, she knew what he would be in Europe. In this she pursued a logical line of thought, which was, if anything, too unsympathetic with the energies and religions of the East. Every other country, one may say, has been an ally of the Turk; that is, of the Mongol and the Moslem. The French played them as pieces against Austria; the English warmly supported them under the Palmerston regime; even the young Italians sent troops to the Crimea; and of Prussia and her Austrian vassal it is nowadays needless to speak. For good or evil, it is the fact of history that Russia is the only Power in Europe that has never supported the Crescent against the Cross.

That, doubtless, will appear an unimportant matter; but it may become important under certain peculiar conditions. Suppose, for the sake of argument, that there were a powerful prince in Europe who had gone ostentatiously out of his way to pay reverence to the remains of the Tartar, Mongol and Moslem, which are left as outposts in Europe. Suppose there were a Christian Emperor who could not even go to the tomb of the Crucified, without pausing to congratulate the last and living crucifier. If there were an Emperor who gave guns and guides and maps and drill instructors to defend the remains of the Mongol in Christendom, what should we say to him? I think at least we might ask him what he meant by his impudence, when he talked about supporting a semi-oriental power. That we support a semi-oriental power we deny. That he has supported an entirely oriental power cannot be denied—no, not even by the man who did it.

But here is to be noted the essential difference between Russia and Prussia; especially by those who use the ordinary Liberal arguments against the latter. Russia has a policy which she pursues, if you will, through evil and good; but at least so as to produce good as well as evil. Let it be granted that the policy has made her oppressive to the Finns and the Poles— though the Russian Poles feel far less oppressed than do the Prussian Poles. But it is a mere historic fact, that if Russia has been a despot to some small nations, she has been a deliverer to others. She did, so far as in her lay, emancipate the Servians and the Montenegrins. But whom did Prussia ever emancipate— even by accident? It is indeed somewhat extraordinary that in the perpetual permutations of international politics, the Hohenzollerns have never gone astray into the path of enlightenment. They have been in alliance with almost everybody off and on: with France, with England, with Austria, with Russia. Can anyone candidly say that they have left on any one of these people the faintest impress of progress or liberation? Prussia was the enemy of the French Monarchy; but a worse enemy of the French Revolution. Prussia had been an enemy of the Czar; but she was a worse enemy of the Duma. Prussia totally disregarded Austrian rights: but she is to-day quite ready to inflict Austrian wrongs. This is the strong particular difference between the one empire and the other. Russia is pursuing certain intelligible and sincere ends, which to her at least are ideals, and for which, therefore, she will make sacrifices and will protect the weak. But the North German soldier is a sort of abstract tyrant, everywhere and always on the side of materialistic tyranny. This Teuton in uniform has been found in strange places; shooting farmers before Saratoga and flogging soldiers in Surrey, hanging niggers in Africa and raping girls in Wicklow; but never, by some mysterious fatality, lending a hand to the freeing of a single city or the independence of one solitary flag. Wherever scorn and prosperous oppression are, there is the Prussian; unconsciously consistent, instinctively restrictive, innocently evil; "following darkness like a dream."

Suppose we heard of a person (gifted with some longevity) who had helped Alva to persecute Dutch Protestants, then helped Cromwell to persecute Irish Catholics, and then helped Claverhouse to persecute Scotch Puritans, we should find it rather easier to call him a persecutor than to call him a Protestant or a Catholic. Curiously enough this is actually the position in which the Prussian stands in Europe. No argument can alter the fact that in three converging and conclusive cases, he has been on the side of three distinct rulers of different religions, who had nothing whatever in common except that they were ruling oppressively. In these three Governments, taken separately, one can see something excusable or at least human. When the Kaiser encouraged the Russian rulers to crush the Revolution, the Russian rulers undoubtedly believed they were wrestling with an inferno of atheism and anarchy. A Socialist of the ordinary English kind cried out upon me when I spoke of Stolypin, and said he was chiefly known by the halter called "Stolypin's Necktie." As a fact, there were many other things interesting about Stolypin besides his necktie: his policy of peasant proprietorship, his extraordinary personal courage, and certainly none more interesting than that movement in his death agony, when he made the sign of the cross towards the Czar, as the crown and captain of his Christianity. But the Kaiser does not regard the Czar as the captain of Christianity. Far from it. What he supported in Stolypin was the necktie and nothing but the necktie: the gallows and not the cross. The Russian ruler did believe that the Orthodox Church was orthodox. The Austrian Archduke did really desire to make the Catholic Church catholic. He did really believe that he was being Pro-Catholic in being Pro-Austrian. But the Kaiser cannot be Pro-Catholic, and therefore cannot have been really Pro-Austrian, he was simply and solely Anti-Servian. Nay, even in the cruel and sterile strength of Turkey, anyone with imagination can see something of the tragedy and therefore of the tenderness of true belief. The worst that can be said of the Moslems is, as the poet put it, they offered to man the choice of the Koran or the sword. The best that can be said for the German is that he does not care about the Koran, but is satisfied if he can have the sword. And for me, I confess, even the sins of these three other striving empires take on, in comparison, something that is sorrowful and dignified: and I feel they do not deserve that this little Lutheran lounger should patronise all that is evil in them, while ignoring all that is good. He is not Catholic, he is not Orthodox, he is not Mahomedan. He is merely an old gentleman who wishes to share the crime though he cannot share the creed. He desires to be a persecutor by the pang without the palm. So strongly do all the instincts of the Prussian drive against liberty, that he would rather oppress other people's subjects than think of anybody going without the benefits of oppression. He is a sort of disinterested despot. He is as disinterested as the devil who is ready to do anyone's dirty work.

This would seem obviously fantastic were it not supported by solid facts which cannot be explained otherwise. Indeed it would be inconceivable if we were thinking of a whole people, consisting of free and varied individuals. But in Prussia the governing class is really a governing class: and a very few people are needed to think along these lines to make all the other people act along them. And the paradox of Prussia is this: that while its princes and nobles have no other aim on this earth but to destroy democracy wherever it shows itself, they have contrived to get themselves trusted, not as wardens of the past but as forerunners of the future. Even they cannot believe that their theory is popular, but they do believe that it is progressive. Here again we find the spiritual chasm between the two monarchies in question. The Russian institutions are, in many cases, really left in the rear of the Russian people, and many of the Russian people know it. But the Prussian institutions are supposed to be in advance of the Prussian people, and most of the Prussian people believe it. It is thus much easier for the war-lords to go everywhere and impose a hopeless slavery upon everyone, for they have already imposed a sort of hopeful slavery on their own simple race.

And when men shall speak to us of the hoary iniquities of Russia and of how antiquated is the Russian system, we shall answer "Yes; that is the superiority of Russia." Their institutions are part of their history, whether as relics or fossils. Their abuses have really been uses: that is to say, they have been used up. If they have old engines of terror or torment, they may fall to pieces from mere rust, like an old coat of armour. But in the case of the Prussian tyranny, if it be tyranny at all, it is the whole point of its claim that it is not antiquated, but just going to begin, like the showman. Prussia has a whole thriving factory of thumbscrews, a whole humming workshop of wheels and racks, of the newest and neatest pattern, with which to win back Europe to the Reaction ... *infandum renovare dolorem* And if we wish to test the truth of this, it can be done by the same method which showed us that Russia, if her race or religion could sometimes make her an invader and an oppressor, could also be made an emancipator and a knight errant. In the same way, if the Russian institutions are old-fashioned, they honestly exhibit the good as well as the bad that can be found in old-fashioned things.

In their police system they have an inequality which is against our ideas of law. But in their commune system they have an equality that is older than law itself. Even when they flogged each other like barbarians, they called upon each other by their Christian names like children. At their worst they retained all the best of a rude society. At their best, they are simply good, like good children or good nuns. But in Prussia, all that is best in the civilised machinery is put at the service of all that is worst in the barbaric mind. Here again the Prussian has no accidental merits, none of those lucky survivals, none of those late repentances, which make the patchwork glory of Russia. Here all is sharpened to a point and pointed to a purpose, and that purpose, if words and acts have any meaning at all, is the destruction of liberty throughout the world.

IV. THE ESCAPE OF FOLLY

In considering the Prussian point of view, we have been considering what seems to be mainly a mental limitation: a kind of knot in the brain. Towards the problem of Slav population, of English colonisation, of French armies and reinforcements, it shows the same strange philosophic sulks. So far as I can follow it, it seems to amount to saying "It is very wrong that you should be superior to me, because I am superior to you." The spokesmen of this system seem to have a curious capacity for concentrating this entanglement or contradiction, sometimes into a single paragraph, or even a single sentence. I have already referred to the German Emperor's celebrated suggestion that in order to avert the peril of Hunnishness we should all become Huns. A much stronger instance is his more recent order to his troops touching the war in Northern France. As most people know, his words ran "It is my Royal and Imperial command that you concentrate your energies, for the immediate present, upon one single purpose, and that is that you address all your skill and all the valour of my soldiers to exterminate first the treacherous English and to walk over General French's contemptible little army." The rudeness of the remark an Englishman can afford to pass over; what I am interested in is the mentality, the train of thought that can manage to entangle itself even in so brief a space. If French's little Army is contemptible, it would seem clear that all the skill and valour of the German Army had better not be concentrated on it, but on the larger and less contemptible allies. If all the skill and valour of the German Army are concentrated on it, it is not being treated as contemptible. But the Prussian rhetorician had two incompatible sentiments in his mind; and he insisted on saying them both at once. He wanted to think of an English Army as a small thing; but he also wanted to think of an English defeat as a big thing. He wanted to exult, at the same moment, in the utter weakness of the British in their attack; and the supreme skill and valour of the Germans in repelling such an attack. Somehow it must be made a common and obvious collapse for England; and yet a daring and unexpected triumph for Germany. In trying to express these contradictory conceptions simultaneously, he got rather mixed.

Therefore he bade Germania fill all her vales and mountains with the dying agonies of this almost invisible earwig; and let the impure blood of this cockroach redden the Rhine down to the sea.

But it would be unfair to base the criticism on the utterance of any accidental and hereditary prince: and it is quite equally clear in the case of the philosophers who have been held up to us, even in England, as the very prophets of progress. And in nothing is it shown more sharply than in the curious confused talk about Race and especially about the Teutonic Race. Professor Harnack and similar people are reproaching us, I understand, for having broken "the bond of Teutonism": a bond which the Prussians have strictly observed both in breach and observance. We note it in their open annexation of lands wholly inhabited by negroes, such as Denmark. We note it equally in their instant and joyful recognition of the flaxen hair and light blue eyes of the Turks. But it is still the abstract principle of Professor Harnack which interests me most; and in following it I have the same complexity of inquiry, but the same simplicity of result. Comparing the Professor's concern about "Teutonism" with his unconcern about Belgium, I can only reach the following result: "A man need not keep a promise he has made. But a man must keep a promise he has not made." There certainly was a treaty binding Britain to Belgium; if it was only a scrap of paper. If there was any treaty binding Britain to Teutonism it is, to say the least of it, a lost scrap of paper; almost what one would call a scrap of waste-paper. Here again the pedants under consideration exhibit the illogical perversity that makes the brain reel. There is obligation and there is no obligation: sometimes it appears that Germany and England must keep faith with each other; sometimes that Germany need not keep faith with anybody and anything; sometimes that we alone among European peoples are almost entitled to be Germans; sometimes that besides us, Russians and Frenchmen almost rise to a Germanic loveliness of character. But through all there is, hazy but not hypocritical, this sense of some common Teutonism.

Professor Haeckel, another of the witnesses raised up against us, attained to some celebrity at one time through proving the remarkable resemblance between two different things by printing duplicate pictures of the same thing. Professor Haeckel's contribution to biology, in this case, was exactly like Professor Harnack's contribution to ethnology. Professor Harnack knows what a German is like. When he wants to imagine what an Englishman is like, he simply photographs the same German over again. In both cases there is probably sincerity as well as simplicity. Haeckel was so certain that the species illustrated in embryo really are closely related and linked up, that it seemed to him a small thing to simplify it by mere repetition. Harnack is so certain that the German and Englishman are almost alike, that he really risks the generalisation that they are exactly alike. He photographs, so to speak, the same fair and foolish face twice over; and calls it a remarkable resemblance between cousins. Thus, he can prove the existence of Teutonism just about as conclusively as Haeckel has proved the more tenable proposition of the non-existence of God.

Now the German and the Englishman are not in the least alike—except in the sense that neither of them are negroes. They are, in everything good and evil, more unlike than any other two men we can take at random from the great European family. They are opposite from the roots of their history, nay of their geography. It is an understatement to call Britain insular. Britain is not only an island, but an island slashed by the sea till it nearly splits into three islands; and even the Midlands can almost smell the salt. Germany is a powerful, beautiful and fertile inland country, which can only find the sea by one or two twisted and narrow paths, as people find a subterranean lake. Thus the British Navy is really national because it is natural; it has cohered out of hundreds of accidental adventures of ships and shipmen before Chaucer's time and after it. But the German Navy is an artificial thing; as artificial as a constructed Alp would be in England. William II. has simply copied the British Navy as Frederick II. copied the French Army: and this Japanese or ant-like assiduity in imitation is one of the hundred qualities which the Germans have and the English markedly have not. There are other German superiorities which are very much superior.

The one or two really jolly things that the Germans have got are precisely the things which the English haven't got: notably a real habit of popular music and of the ancient songs of the people, not merely spreading from the towns or caught from the professionals. In this the Germans rather resemble the Welsh; though heaven knows what becomes of Teutonism if they do. But the difference between the Germans and the English goes deeper than all these signs of it; they differ more than any other two Europeans in the normal posture of the mind. Above all, they differ in what is the most English of all English traits; that shame which the French may be right in calling "the bad shame"; for it is certainly mixed up with pride and suspicion, the upshot of which we called shyness. Even an Englishman's rudeness is often rooted in his being embarrassed. But a German's rudeness is rooted in his never being embarrassed. He eats and makes love noisily. He never feels a speech or a song or a sermon or a large meal to be what the English call "out of place" in particular circumstances. When Germans are patriotic and religious, they have no reaction against patriotism and religion as have the English and the French.

Nay, the mistake of Germany in the modern disaster largely arose from the facts that she thought England was simple, when England is very subtle. She thought that because our politics have become largely financial that they had become wholly financial; that because our aristocrats had become pretty cynical that they had become entirely corrupt. They could not seize the subtlety by which a rather used-up English gentleman might sell a coronet when he would not sell a fortress; might lower the public standards and yet refuse to lower the flag.

In short, the Germans are quite sure that they understand us entirely, because they do not understand us at all. Possibly if they began to understand us they might hate us even more: but I would rather be hated for some small but real reason, than pursued with love on account of all kinds of qualities which I do not possess and which I do not desire. And when the Germans get their first genuine glimpse of what modern England is like, they will discover that England has a very broken, belated and inadequate sense of having an obligation to Europe, but no sort of sense whatever of having any obligation to Teutonism.

This is the last and strongest of the Prussian qualities we have here considered. There is in stupidity of this sort a strange slippery strength: because it can be not only outside rules but outside reason. The man who really cannot see that he is contradicting himself has a great advantage in controversy; though the advantage breaks down when he tries to reduce it to simple addition, to chess, or to the game called war. It is the same about the stupidity of the one-sided kinship. The drunkard who is quite certain that a total stranger is his long-lost brother, has a greater advantage until it comes to matters of detail. "We must have chaos within," said Nietzsche, "that we may give birth to a dancing star."

In these slight notes I have suggested the principal strong points of the Prussian character. A failure in honour which almost amounts to a failure in memory: an egomania that is honestly blind to the fact that the other party is an ego; and, above all, an actual itch for tyranny and interference, the devil which everywhere torments the idle and the proud. To these must be added a certain mental shapelessness which can expand or contract without reference to reason or record; a potential infinity of excuses. If the English had been on the German side, the German professors would have noted what irresistible energies had evolved the Teutons. As the English are on the other side, the German professors will say that these Teutons were not sufficiently evolved. Or they will say that they were just sufficiently evolved to show that they were not Teutons. Probably they will say both. But the truth is that all that they call evolution should rather be called evasion. They tell us they are opening windows of enlightenment and doors of progress. The truth is that they are breaking up the whole house of the human intellect, that they may abscond in any direction. There is an ominous and almost monstrous parallel between the position of their over-rated philosophers and of their comparatively under-rated soldiers. For what their professors call roads of progress are really routes of escape.

Utopia of Usurers and Other Essays

By

Gilbert Keith Chesterton

CONTENTS

A SONG OF SWORDS

*"A drove of cattle came into a village called Swords;
and was stopped by the rioters."—Daily Paper.*

*In the place called Swords on the Irish road
It is told for a new renown
How we held the horns of the cattle, and how
We will hold the horns of the devils now
Ere the lord of hell with the horn on his brow
Is crowned in Dublin town.*

*Light in the East and light in the West,
And light on the cruel lords,
On the souls that suddenly all men knew,
And the green flag flew and the red flag flew,
And many a wheel of the world stopped, too,
When the cattle were stopped at Swords.*

*Be they sinners or less than saints
That smite in the street for rage,
We know where the shame shines bright; we know
You that they smite at, you their foe,
Lords of the lawless wage and low,
This is your lawful wage.*

*You pinched a child to a torture price
That you dared not name in words;
So black a jest was the silver bit
That your own speech shook for the shame of it,
And the coward was plain as a cow they hit
When the cattle have strayed at Swords.*

*The wheel of the torrent of wives went round
To break men's brotherhood;
You gave the good Irish blood to grease
The clubs of your country's enemies;
you saw the brave man beat to the knees:
And you saw that it was good.*

The rope of the rich is long and long—
The longest of hangmen's cords;
But the kings and crowds are holding their breath,
In a giant shadow o'er all beneath
Where God stands holding the scales of Death
Between the cattle and Swords.

Haply the lords that hire and lend
The lowest of all men's lords,
Who sell their kind like kine at a fair,
Will find no head of their cattle there;
But faces of men where cattle were:
Faces of men—and Swords.

UTOPIA OF USURERS

I. ART AND ADVERTISEMENT

I propose, subject to the patience of the reader, to devote two or three articles to prophecy. Like all healthy-minded prophets, sacred and profane, I can only prophesy when I am in a rage and think things look ugly for everybody. And like all healthy-minded prophets, I prophesy in the hope that my prophecy may not come true. For the prediction made by the true soothsayer is like the warning given by a good doctor. And the doctor has really triumphed when the patient he condemned to death has revived to life. The threat is justified at the very moment when it is falsified. Now I have said again and again (and I shall continue to say again and again on all the most inappropriate occasions) that we must hit Capitalism, and hit it hard, for the plain and definite reason that it is growing stronger. Most of the excuses which serve the capitalists as masks are, of course, the excuses of hypocrites. They lie when they claim philanthropy; they no more feel any particular love of men than Albu felt an affection for Chinamen. They lie when they say they have reached their position through their own organising ability. They generally have to pay men to organise the mine, exactly as they pay men to go down it. They often lie about the present wealth, as they generally lie about their past poverty. But when they say that they are going in for a "constructive social policy," they do not lie. They really are going in for a constructive social policy. And we must go in for an equally destructive social policy; and destroy, while it is still half-constructed, the accursed thing which they construct.

The Example of the Arts

Now I propose to take, one after another, certain aspects and departments of modern life, and describe what I think they will be like in this paradise of plutocrats, this Utopia of gold and brass in which the great story of England seems so likely to end. I propose to say what I think our new masters, the mere millionaires, will do with certain human interests and institutions, such as art, science, jurisprudence, or religion—unless we strike soon enough to prevent them. And for the sake of argument I will take in this article the example of the arts.

Most people have seen a picture called "Bubbles," which is used for the advertisement of a celebrated soap, a small cake of which is introduced into the pictorial design. And anybody with an instinct for design (the caricaturist of the Daily Herald, for instance), will guess that it was not originally a part of the design. He will see that the cake of soap destroys the picture as a picture; as much as if the cake of soap had been used to Scrub off the paint. Small as it is, it breaks and confuses the whole balance of objects in the composition. I offer no judgment here upon Millais's action in the matter; in fact, I do not know what it was. The important point for me at the moment is that the picture was not painted for the soap, but the soap added to the picture. And the spirit of the corrupting change which has separated us from that Victorian epoch can be best seen in this: that the Victorian atmosphere, with all its faults, did not permit such a style of patronage to pass as a matter of course. Michael Angelo may have been proud to have helped an emperor or a pope; though, indeed, I think he was prouder than they were on his own account. I do not believe Sir John Millais was proud of having helped a soap-boiler. I do not say he thought it wrong; but he was not proud of it. And that marks precisely the change from his time to our own. Our merchants have really adopted the style of merchant princes. They have begun openly to dominate the civilisation of the State, as the emperors and popes openly dominated in Italy. In Millais's time, broadly speaking, art was supposed to mean good art; advertisement was supposed to mean inferior art. The head of a black man, painted to advertise somebody's blacking, could be a rough symbol, like an inn sign. The black man had only to be black enough. An artist exhibiting the picture of a negro was expected to know that a black man is not so black as he is painted. He was expected to render a thousand tints of grey and brown and violet: for there is no such thing as a black man just as there is no such thing as a white man. A fairly clear line separated advertisement from art.

The First Effect
I should say the first effect of the triumph of the capitalist (if we allow him to triumph) will be that that line of demarcation will entirely disappear. There will be no art that might not just

as well be advertisement. I do not necessarily mean that there will be no good art; much of it might be, much of it already is, very good art. You may put it, if you please, in the form that there has been a vast improvement in advertisements. Certainly there would be nothing surprising if the head of a negro advertising Somebody's Blacking now adays were finished with as careful and subtle colours as one of the old and superstitious painters would have wasted on the negro king who brought gifts to Christ. But the improvement of advertisements is the degradation of artists. It is their degradation for this clear and vital reason: that the artist will work, not only to please the rich, but only to increase their riches; which is a considerable step lower. After all, it was as a human being that a pope took pleasure in a cartoon of Raphael or a prince took pleasure in a statuette of Cellini. The prince paid for the statuette; but he did not expect the statuette to pay him. It is my impression that no cake of soap can be found anywhere in the cartoons which the Pope ordered of Raphael. And no one who knows the small-minded cynicism of our plutocracy, its secrecy, its gambling spirit, its contempt of conscience, can doubt that the artist-advertiser will often be assisting enterprises over which he will have no moral control, and of which he could feel no moral approval. He will be working to spread quack medicines, queer investments; and will work for Marconi instead of Medici. And to this base ingenuity he will have to bend the proudest and purest of the virtues of the intellect, the power to attract his brethren, and the noble duty of praise. For that picture by Millais is a very allegorical picture. It is almost a prophecy of what uses are awaiting the beauty of the child unborn. The praise will be of a kind that may correctly be called soap; and the enterprises of a kind that may truly be described as Bubbles.

II. LETTERS AND THE NEW LAUREATES

In these articles I only take two or three examples of the first and fundamental fact of our time. I mean the fact that the capitalists of our community are becoming quite openly the kings of it. In my last (and first) article, I took the case of Art and advertisement. I pointed out that Art must be growing worse—merely because advertisement is growing better. In those days Millais condescended to Pears' soap. In these days I really think it would be Pears who condescended to Millais. But here I turn to an art I know more about, that of journalism. Only in my ease the art verges on artlessness.

The great difficulty with the English lies in the absence of something one may call democratic imagination. We find it easy to realise an individual, but very hard to realise that the great masses consist of individuals. Our system has been aristocratic: in the special sense of there being only a few actors on the stage. And the back scene is kept quite dark, though it is really a throng of faces. Home Rule tended to be not so much the Irish as the Grand Old Man. The Boer War tended not to be so much South Africa as simply "Joe." And it is the amusing but distressing fact that every class of political leadership, as it comes to the front in its turn, catches the rays of this isolating lime-light; and becomes a small aristocracy. Certainly no one has the aristocratic complaint so badly as the Labour Party. At the recent Congress, the real difference between Larkin and the English Labour leaders was not so much in anything right or wrong in what he said, as in something elemental and even mystical in the way he suggested a mob. But it must be plain, even to those who agree with the more official policy, that for Mr. Havelock Wilson the principal question was Mr. Havelock Wilson; and that Mr. Sexton was mainly considering the dignity and fine feelings of Mr. Sexton. You may say they were as sensitive as aristocrats, or as sulky as babies; the point is that the feeling was personal. But Larkin, like Danton, not only talks like ten thousand men talking, but he also has some of the carelessness of the colossus of Arcis; "Que mon nom soit fletri, que la France soit libre."

A Dance of Degradation

It is needless to say that this respecting of persons has led all the other parties a dance of degradation. We ruin South Africa because it would be a slight on Lord Gladstone to save South Africa. We have a bad army, because it would be a snub to Lord Haldane to have a good army. And no Tory is allowed to say "Marconi" for fear Mr. George should say "Kynoch." But this curious personal element, with its appalling lack of patriotism, has appeared in a new and curious form in another department of life; the department of literature, especially periodical literature. And the form it takes is the next example I shall give of the way in which the capitalists are now appearing, more and more openly, as the masters and princes of the community.

I will take a Victorian instance to mark the change; as I did in the case of the advertisement of "Bubbles." It was said in my childhood, by the more apoplectic and elderly sort of Tory, that W. E. Gladstone was only a Free Trader because he had a partnership in Gilbey's foreign wines. This was, no doubt, nonsense; but it had a dim symbolic, or mainly prophetic, truth in it. It was true, to some extent even then, and it has been increasingly true since, that the statesman was often an ally of the salesman; and represented not only a nation of shopkeepers, but one particular shop. But in Gladstone's time, even if this was true, it was never the whole truth; and no one would have endured it being the admitted truth. The politician was not solely an eloquent and persuasive bagman travelling for certain business men; he was bound to mix even his corruption with some intelligible ideals and rules of policy. And the proof of it is this: that at least it was the statesman who bulked large in the public eye; and his financial backer was entirely in the background. Old gentlemen might choke over their port, with the moral certainty that the Prime Minister had shares in a wine merchant's. But the old gentleman would have died on the spot if the wine merchant had really been made as important as the Prime Minister. If it had been Sir Walter Gilbey whom Disraeli denounced, or Punch caricatured; if Sir Walter Gilbey's favourite collars (with the design of which I am unacquainted) had grown as large as the wings of an archangel; if Sir Walter Gilbey had been credited with successfully eliminating the British Oak with his little hatchet; if, near the Temple and the Courts of Justice, our sight was struck by a majestic statue of a wine merchant; or if the earnest Conservative lady who threw a gingerbread-nut at the Premier had directed it towards the wine merchant instead, the shock to Victorian England would have been very great indeed.

Haloes for Employers

Now something very like that is happening; the mere wealthy employer is beginning to have not only the power but some of the glory. I have seen in several magazines lately, and magazines of a high class, the appearance of a new kind of article. Literary men are being employed to praise a big business man personally, as men used to praise a king. They not only find political reasons for the commercial schemes—that they have done for some time past—they also find moral defences for the commercial schemers. They describe the capitalist's brain of steel and heart of gold in a way that Englishmen hitherto have been at least in the habit of reserving for romantic figures like Garibaldi or Gordon. In one excellent magazine Mr. T. P. O'Connor, who, when he likes, can write on letters like a man of letters, has some purple pages of praise of Sir Joseph Lyons—the man who runs those teashop places. He incidentally brought in a delightful passage about the beautiful souls possessed by some people called Salmon and Gluckstein. I think I like best the passage where he said that Lyons's charming social accomplishments included a talent for "imitating a Jew." The article is accompanied with a large and somewhat leering portrait of that shopkeeper, which makes the parlour-trick in question particularly astonishing. Another literary man, who certainly ought to know better, wrote in another paper a piece of hero-worship about Mr. Selfridge. No doubt the fashion will spread, and the art of words, as polished and pointed by Ruskin or Meredith, will be perfected yet further to explore the labyrinthine heart of Harrod; or compare the simple stoicism of Marshall with the saintly charm of Snelgrove.

Any man can be praised—and rightly praised. If he only stands on two legs he does something a cow cannot do. If a rich man can manage to stand on two legs for a reasonable time, it is called self-control. If he has only one leg, it is called (with some truth) self-sacrifice. I could say something nice (and true) about every man I have ever met. Therefore, I do not doubt I could find something nice about Lyons or Selfridge if I searched for it. But I shall not. The nearest postman or cab-man will provide me with just the same brain of steel and heart of gold as these unlucky lucky men. But I do resent the whole age of patronage being revived under such absurd patrons; and all poets becoming court poets, under kings that have taken no oath, nor led us into any battle.

III. UNBUSINESSLIKE BUSINESS

The fairy tales we were all taught did not, like the history we were all taught, consist entirely of lies. Parts of the tale of "Puss in Boots" or "Jack and the Beanstalk" may strike the realistic eye as a little unlikely and out of the common way, so to speak; but they contain some very solid and very practical truths. For instance, it may be noted that both in "Puss in Boots" and "Jack and the Beanstalk" if I remember aright, the ogre was not only an ogre but also a magician. And it will generally be found that in all such popular narratives, the king, if he is a wicked king, is generally also a wizard. Now there is a very vital human truth enshrined in this. Bad government, like good government, is a spiritual thing. Even the tyrant never rules by force alone; but mostly by fairy tales. And so it is with the modern tyrant, the great employer. The sight of a millionaire is seldom, in the ordinary sense, an enchanting sight: nevertheless, he is in his way an enchanter. As they say in the gushing articles about him in the magazines, he is a fascinating personality. So is a snake. At least he is fascinating to rabbits; and so is the millionaire to the rabbit-witted sort of people that ladies and gentlemen have allowed themselves to become. He does, in a manner, cast a spell, such as that which imprisoned princes and princesses under the shapes of falcons or stags. He has truly turned men into sheep, as Circe turned them into swine.

Now, the chief of the fairy tales, by which he gains this glory and glamour, is a certain hazy association he has managed to create between the idea of bigness and the idea of practicality. Numbers of the rabbit-witted ladies and gentlemen do really think, in spite of themselves and their experience, that so long as a shop has hundreds of different doors and a great many hot and unhealthy underground departments (they must be hot; this is very important), and more people than would be needed for a man-of-war, or crowded cathedral, to say: "This way, madam," and "The next article, sir," it follows that the goods are good. In short, they hold that the big businesses are businesslike. They are not. Any housekeeper in a truthful mood, that is to say, any housekeeper in a bad temper, will tell you that they are not. But housekeepers, too, are human, and therefore inconsistent and complex; and they do not always stick to truth and bad temper. They are also affected by this queer idolatry of the enormous and elaborate; and cannot help feeling that anything so complicated must go like clockwork. But complexity is no guarantee of accuracy—in clockwork or in anything else. A clock can be as wrong as the human head; and a clock can stop, as suddenly as the human heart.

But this strange poetry of plutocracy prevails over people against their very senses. You write to one of the great London stores or emporia, asking, let us say, for an umbrella. A month or two afterwards you receive a very elaborately constructed parcel, containing a broken parasol. You are very pleased. You are gratified to reflect on what a vast number of assistants and employees had combined to break that parasol. You luxuriate in the memory of all those long rooms and departments and wonder in which of them the parasol that you never ordered was broken. Or you want a toy elephant for your child on Christmas Day; as children, like all nice and healthy people, are very ritualistic. Some week or so after Twelfth Night, let us say, you have the pleasure of removing three layers of pasteboards, five layers of brown paper, and fifteen layers of tissue paper and discovering the fragments of an artificial crocodile. You smile in an expansive spirit. You feel that your soul has been broadened by the vision of incompetence conducted on so large a scale. You admire all the more the colossal and Omnipresent Brain of the Organiser of Industry, who amid all his multitudinous cares did not disdain to remember his duty of smashing even the smallest toy of the smallest child. Or, supposing you have asked him to send you some two rolls of cocoa-nut matting: and supposing (after a due interval for reflection) he duly delivers to you the five rolls of wire netting. You take pleasure in the consideration of a mystery: which coarse minds might have called a mistake. It consoles you to know how big the business is: and what an enormous number of people were needed to make such a mistake.

That is the romance that has been told about the big shops; in the literature and art which they have bought, and which (as I said in my recent articles) will soon be quite indistinguishable from their ordinary advertisements. The literature is commercial; and it is only fair to say that the commerce is often really literary. It is no romance, but only rubbish.

The big commercial concerns of to-day are quite

exceptionally incompetent. They will be even more incompetent when they are omnipotent. Indeed, that is, and always has been, the whole point of a monopoly; the old and sound argument against a monopoly. It is only because it is incompetent that it has to be omnipotent. When one large shop occupies the whole of one side of a street (or sometimes both sides), it does so in order that men may be unable to get what they want; and may be forced to buy what they don't want. That the rapidly approaching kingdom of the Capitalists will ruin art and letters, I have already said. I say here that in the only sense that can be called human, it will ruin trade, too.

I will not let Christmas go by, even when writing for a revolutionary paper necessarily appealing to many with none of my religious sympathies, without appealing to those sympathies. I knew a man who sent to a great rich shop for a figure for a group of Bethlehem. It arrived broken. I think that is exactly all that business men have now the sense to do.

IV. THE WAR ON HOLIDAYS

The general proposition, not always easy to define exhaustively, that the reign of the capitalist will be the reign of the cad—that is, of the unlicked type that is neither the citizen nor the gentleman—can be excellently studied in its attitude towards holidays. The special emblematic Employer of to-day, especially the Model Employer (who is the worst sort) has in his starved and evil heart a sincere hatred of holidays. I do not mean that he necessarily wants all his workmen to work until they drop; that only occurs when he happens to be stupid as well as wicked. I do not mean to say that he is necessarily unwilling to grant what he would call "decent hours of labour." He may treat men like dirt; but if you want to make money, even out of dirt, you must let it lie fallow by some rotation of rest. He may treat men as dogs, but unless he is a lunatic he will for certain periods let sleeping dogs lie.

But humane and reasonable hours for labour have nothing whatever to do with the idea of holidays. It is not even a question of ten hours day and eight-hours day; it is not a question of cutting down leisure to the space necessary for food, sleep and exercise. If the modern employer came to the conclusion, for some reason or other, that he could get most out of his men by working them hard for only two hours a day, his whole mental attitude would still be foreign and hostile to holidays. For his whole mental attitude is that the passive time and the active time are alike useful for him and his business. All is, indeed, grist that comes to his mill, including the millers. His slaves still serve him in unconsciousness, as dogs still hunt in slumber. His grist is ground not only by the sounding wheels of iron, but by the soundless wheel of blood and brain. His sacks are still filling silently when the doors are shut on the streets and the sound of the grinding is low.

The Great Holiday

Now a holiday has no connection with using a man either by beating or feeding him. When you give a man a holiday you give him back his body and soul. It is quite possible you may be doing him an injury (though he seldom thinks so), but that does not affect the question for those to whom a holiday is holy. Immortality is the great holiday; and a holiday, like the immortality in the old theologies, is a double-edged privilege. But wherever it is genuine it is simply the restoration and completion of the man. If people ever looked at the printed word under their eye, the word "recreation" would be like the word "resurrection," the blast of a trumpet.

A man, being merely useful, is necessarily incomplete, especially if he be a modern man and means by being useful being "utilitarian." A man going into a modern club gives up his hat; a man going into a modern factory gives up his head. He then goes in and works loyally for the old firm to build up the great fabric of commerce (which can be done without a head), but when he has done work he goes to the cloak-room, like the man at the club, and gets his head back again; that is the germ of the holiday. It may be urged that the club man who leaves his hat often goes away with another hat; and perhaps it may be the same with the factory hand who has left his head. A hand that has lost its head may affect the fastidious as a mixed metaphor; but, God pardon us all, what an unmixed truth! We could almost prove the whole ease from the habit of calling human beings merely "hands" while they are working; as if the hand were horribly cut off, like the hand that has offended; as if, while the sinner entered heaven maimed, his unhappy hand still laboured laying up riches for the lords of hell. But to return to the man whom we found waiting for his head in the cloak-room. It may be urged, we say, that he might take the wrong head, like the wrong hat; but here the similarity ceases. For it has been observed by benevolent onlookers at life's drama that the hat taken away by mistake is frequently better than the real hat; whereas the head taken away after the hours of toil is certainly worse: stained with the cobwebs and dust of this dustbin of all the centuries.

The Supreme Adventure

All the words dedicated to places of eating and drinking are pure and poetic words. Even the word "hotel" is the word hospital. And St. Julien, whose claret I drank this Christmas, was the patron saint of innkeepers, because (as far as I can make out) he was hospitable to lepers. Now I do not say that the ordinary hotel-keeper in Piccadilly or the Avenue de l'Opera would embrace a leper, slap him on the back, and ask him to order what he liked; but I do say that hospitality is his trade virtue. And I do also say it is well to keep before our eyes the supreme adventure of a virtue. If you are brave, think of the man who was braver than you. If you are kind, think of the man who was kinder than you.

That is what was meant by having a patron saint. That is the link between the poor saint who received bodily lepers and the great hotel proprietor who (as a rule) receives spiritual lepers. But a word yet weaker than "hotel" illustrates the same point— the word "restaurant." There again you have the admission that there is a definite building or statue to "restore"; that ineffaceable image of man that some call the image of God. And that is the holiday; it is the restaurant or restoring thing that, by a blast of magic, turns a man into himself.

This complete and reconstructed man is the nightmare of the modern capitalist. His whole scheme would crack across like a mirror of Shallot, if once a plain man were ready for his two plain duties—ready to live and ready to die. And that horror of holidays which marks the modern capitalist is very largely a horror of the vision of a whole human being: something that is not a "hand" or a "head for figures." But an awful creature who has met himself in the wilderness. The employers will give time to eat, time to sleep; they are in terror of a time to think.

To anyone who knows any history it is wholly needless to say that holidays have been destroyed. As Mr. Belloc, who knows much more history than you or I, recently pointed out in the "Pall Mall Magazine," Shakespeare's title of "Twelfth Night: or What You Will" simply meant that a winter carnival for everybody went on wildly till the twelfth night after Christmas. Those of my readers who work for modern offices or factories might ask their employers for twelve days' holidays after Christmas. And they might let me know the reply.

V. THE CHURCH OF THE SERVILE STATE

I confess I cannot see why mere blasphemy by itself should be an excuse for tyranny and treason; or how the mere isolated fact of a man not believing in God should be a reason for my believing in Him.

But the rather spinsterish flutter among some of the old Freethinkers has put one tiny ripple of truth in it; and that affects the idea which I wish to emphasise even to monotony in these pages. I mean the idea that the new community which the capitalists are now constructing will be a very complete and absolute community; and one which will tolerate nothing really independent of itself. Now, it is true that any positive creed, true or false, would tend to be independent of itself. It might be Roman Catholicism or Mahomedanism or Materialism; but, if strongly held, it would be a thorn in the side of the Servile State. The Moslem thinks all men immortal: the Materialist thinks all men mortal. But the Moslem does not think the rich Sinbad will live forever; but the poor Sinbad will die on his deathbed. The Materialist does not think that Mr. Haeckel will go to heaven, while all the peasants will go to pot, like their chickens. In every serious doctrine of the destiny of men, there is some trace of the doctrine of the equality of men. But the capitalist really depends on some religion of inequality. The capitalist must somehow distinguish himself from human kind; he must be obviously above it—or he would be obviously below it. Take even the least attractive and popular side of the larger religions to-day; take the mere vetoes imposed by Islam on Atheism or Catholicism. The Moslem veto upon intoxicants cuts across all classes. But it is absolutely necessary for the capitalist (who presides at a Licensing Committee, and also at a large dinner), it is absolutely necessary for him, to make a distinction between gin and champagne. The Atheist veto upon all miracles cuts across all classes. But it is absolutely necessary for the capitalist to make a distinction between his wife (who is an aristocrat and consults crystal gazers and star gazers in the West End), and vulgar miracles claimed by gipsies or travelling showmen. The Catholic veto upon usury, as defined in dogmatic councils, cuts across all classes. But it is absolutely necessary to the capitalist to distinguish more delicately between two kinds of usury; the kind he finds useful and the kind he does not find useful. The religion of the Servile State must have no dogmas or definitions. It cannot afford to have any definitions. For definitions are very dreadful things: they do the two things that most men, especially comfortable men, cannot endure. They fight; and they fight fair.

Every religion, apart from open devil worship, must appeal to a virtue or the pretence of a virtue. But a virtue, generally speaking, does some good to everybody. It is therefore necessary to distinguish among the people it was meant to benefit those whom it does benefit. Modern broad-mindedness benefits the rich; and benefits nobody else. It was meant to benefit the rich; and meant to benefit nobody else. And if you think this unwarranted, I will put before you one plain question. There are some pleasures of the poor that may also mean profits for the rich: there are other pleasures of the poor which cannot mean profits for the rich? Watch this one contrast, and you will watch the whole creation of a careful slavery.

In the last resort the two things called Beer and Soap end only in a froth. They are both below the high notice of a real religion. But there is just this difference: that the soap makes the factory more satisfactory, while the beer only makes the workman more satisfied. Wait and see if the Soap does not increase and the Beer decrease. Wait and see whether the religion of the Servile State is not in every case what I say: the encouragement of small virtues supporting capitalism, the discouragement of the huge virtues that defy it. Many great religions, Pagan and Christian, have insisted on wine. Only one, I think, has insisted on Soap. You will find it in the New Testament attributed to the Pharisees.

VI. SCIENCE AND THE EUGENISTS

The key fact in the new development of plutocracy is that it will use its own blunder as an excuse for further crimes. Everywhere the very completeness of the impoverishment will be made a reason for the enslavement; though the men who impoverished were the same who enslaved. It is as if a highwayman not only took away a gentleman's horse and all his money, but then handed him over to the police for tramping without visible means of subsistence. And the most monstrous feature in this enormous meanness may be noted in the plutocratic appeal to science, or, rather, to the pseudo-science that they call Eugenics.

The Eugenists get the ear of the humane but rather hazy cliques by saying that the present "conditions" under which people work and breed are bad for the race; but the modern mind will not generally stretch beyond one step of reasoning, and the consequence which appears to follow on the consideration of these "conditions" is by no means what would originally have been expected. If somebody says: "A rickety cradle may mean a rickety baby," the natural deduction, one would think, would be to give the people a good cradle, or give them money enough to buy one. But that means higher wages and greater equalisation of wealth; and the plutocratic scientist, with a slightly troubled expression, turns his eyes and pince-nez in another direction. Reduced to brutal terms of truth, his difficulty is this and simply this: More food, leisure, and money for the workman would mean a better workman, better even from the point of view of anyone for whom he worked. But more food, leisure, and money would also mean a more independent workman. A house with a decent fire and a full pantry would be a better house to make a chair or mend a clock in, even from the customer's point of view, than a hovel with a leaky roof and a cold hearth. But a house with a decent fire and a full pantry would also be a better house in which to refuse to make a chair or mend a clock—a much better house to do nothing in—and doing nothing is sometimes one of the highest of the duties of man. All but the hard-hearted must be torn with pity for this pathetic dilemma of the rich man, who has to keep the poor man just stout enough to do the work and just thin enough to have to do it. As he stood gazing at the leaky roof and the rickety cradle in a pensive manner, there one day came into his mind a new and curious idea—one of the most strange, simple, and horrible ideas that have ever risen from the deep pit of original sin.

The roof could not be mended, or, at least, it could not be mended much, without upsetting the capitalist balance, or, rather, disproportion in society; for a man with a roof is a man with a house, and to that extent his house is his castle. The cradle could not be made to rock easier, or, at least, not much easier, without strengthening the hands of the poor household, for the hand that rocks the cradle rules the world—to that extent. But it occurred to the capitalist that there was one sort of furniture in the house that could be altered. The husband and wife could be altered. Birth costs nothing, except in pain and valour and such old-fashioned things; and the merchant need pay no more for mating a strong miner to a healthy fishwife than he pays when the miner mates himself with a less robust female whom he has the sentimentality to prefer. Thus it might be possible, by keeping on certain broad lines of heredity, to have some physical improvement without any moral, political, or social improvement. It might be possible to keep a supply of strong and healthy slaves without coddling them with decent conditions. As the mill-owners use the wind and the water to drive their mills, they would use this natural force as something even cheaper; and turn their wheels by diverting from its channel the blood of a man in his youth. That is what Eugenics means; and that is all that it means.

Of the moral state of those who think of such things it does not become us to speak. The practical question is rather the intellectual one: of whether their calculations are well founded, and whether the men of science can or will guarantee them any such physical certainties. Fortunately, it becomes clearer every day that they are, scientifically speaking, building on the shifting sand. The theory of breeding slaves breaks down through what a democrat calls the equality of men, but which even an oligarchist will find himself forced to call the similarity of men. That is, that though it is not true that all men are normal, it is overwhelmingly certain that most men are normal. All the common Eugenic arguments are drawn from extreme cases, which, even if human honour and laughter allowed of their being eliminated, would not by their elimination greatly affect the mass. For the rest, there remains the enormous weakness in Eugenics, that if ordinary men's judgment or liberty is to be discounted in relation to heredity, the judgment of the judges must be discounted in relation to their heredity. The Eugenic professor may or may not succeed in choosing a baby's parents; it is quite certain that he cannot succeed in choosing his own parents. All his thoughts, including his Eugenic thoughts, are, by the very principle of those thoughts, flowing from a doubtful or tainted source. In short, we should need a perfectly Wise Man to do the thing at all. And if he were a Wise Man he would not do it.

VII. THE EVOLUTION OF THE PRISON

I have never understood why it is that those who talk most about evolution, and talk it in the very age of fashionable evolutionism, do not see the one way in which evolution really does apply to our modern difficulty. There is, of course, an element of evolutionism in the universe; and I know no religion or philosophy that ever entirely ignored it. Evolution, popularly speaking, is that which happens to unconscious things. They grow unconsciously; or fade unconsciously; or rather, some parts of them grow and some parts of them fade; and at any given moment there is almost always some presence of the fading thing, and some incompleteness in the growing one. Thus, if I went to sleep for a hundred years, like the Sleeping Beauty (I wish I could), I should grow a beard—unlike the Sleeping Beauty. And just as I should grow hair if I were asleep, I should grow grass if I were dead. Those whose religion it was that God was asleep were perpetually impressed and affected by the fact that he had a long beard. And those whose philosophy it is that the universe is dead from the beginning (being the grave of nobody in particular) think that is the way that grass can grow. In any case, these developments only occur with dead or dreaming things. What happens when everyone is asleep is called Evolution. What happens when everyone is awake is called Revolution.

There was once an honest man, whose name I never knew, but whose face I can almost see (it is framed in Victorian whiskers and fixed in a Victorian neck-cloth), who was balancing the achievements of France and England in civilisation and social efficiencies. And when he came to the religious aspect he said that there were more stone and brick churches used in France; but, on the other hand, there are more sects in England. Whether such a lively disintegration is a proof of vitality in any valuable sense I have always doubted. The sun may breed maggots in a dead dog; but it is essential for such a liberation of life that the dog should be unconscious or (to say the least of it) absent-minded. Broadly speaking, you may call the thing corruption, if you happen to like dogs. You may call it evolution, if you happen to like maggots. In either case, it is what happens to things if you leave them alone.

The Evolutionists' Error

Now, the modern Evolutionists have made no real use of the idea of evolution, especially in the matter of social prediction. They always fall into what is (from their logical point of view) the error of supposing that evolution knows what it is doing. They predict the State of the future as a fruit rounded and polished. But the whole point of evolution (the only point there is in it) is that no State will ever be rounded and polished, because it will always contain some organs that outlived their use, and some that have not yet fully found theirs. If we wish to prophesy what will happen, we must imagine things now moderate grown enormous; things now local grown universal; things now promising grown triumphant; primroses bigger than sunflowers, and sparrows stalking about like flamingoes.

In other words, we must ask what modern institution has a future before it? What modern institution may have swollen to six times its present size in the social heat and growth of the future? I do not think the Garden City will grow: but of that I may speak in my next and last article of this series. I do not think even the ordinary Elementary School, with its compulsory education, will grow. Too many unlettered people hate the teacher for teaching; and too many lettered people hate the teacher for not teaching. The Garden City will not bear much blossom; the young idea will not shoot, unless it shoots the teacher. But the one flowering tree on the estate, the one natural expansion which I think will expand, is the institution we call the Prison.

Prisons for All

If the capitalists are allowed to erect their constructive capitalist community, I speak quite seriously when I say that I think Prison will become an almost universal experience. It will not necessarily be a cruel or shameful experience: on these points (I concede certainly for the present purpose of debate) it may be a vastly improved experience. The conditions in the prison, very possibly, will be made more humane. But the prison will be made more humane only in order to contain more of humanity. I think little of the judgment and sense of humour of any man who can have watched recent police trials without realising that it is no longer a question of whether the law has been broken by a crime; but, now, solely a question of whether the situation could be mended by an imprisonment. It was so with Tom Mann; it was so with Larkin; it was so with the poor atheist who was kept in gaol for saying something he had been acquitted of saying: it is so in such cases day by day. We no longer lock a man up for doing something; we lock him up in the hope of his doing nothing. Given this principle, it is evidently possible to make the mere conditions of punishment more moderate, or—(more probably) more secret. There may really be more mercy in the Prison, on condition that there is less justice in the Court. I should not be surprised if, before we are done with all this, a man was allowed to smoke in prison, on condition, of course, that he had been put in prison for smoking.

Now that is the process which, in the absence of democratic protest, will certainly proceed, will increase and multiply and replenish the earth and subdue it. Prison may even lose its disgrace for a little time: it will be difficult to make it disgraceful when men like Larkin can be imprisoned for no reason at all, just as his celebrated ancestor was hanged for no reason at all. But capitalist society, which naturally does not know the meaning of honour, cannot know the meaning of disgrace: and it will still go on imprisoning for no reason at all. Or rather for that rather simple reason that makes a cat spring or a rat run away.

It matters little whether our masters stoop to state the matter in the form that every prison should be a school; or in the more candid form that every school should be a prison. They have already fulfilled their servile principle in the case of the schools. Everyone goes to the Elementary Schools except the few people who tell them to go there. I prophesy that (unless our revolt succeeds) nearly everyone will be going to Prison, with a precisely similar patience.

VIII. THE LASH FOR LABOUR

If I were to prophesy that two hundred years hence a grocer would have the right and habit of beating the grocer's assistant with a stick, or that shop girls might be flogged, as they already can be fined, many would regard it as rather a rash remark. It would be a rash remark. Prophecy is always unreliable; unless we except the kind which is avowedly irrational, mystical and supernatural prophecy. But relatively to nearly all the other prophecies that are being made around me to-day, I should say my prediction stood an exceptionally good chance. In short, I think the grocer with the stick is a figure we are far more likely to see than the Superman or the Samurai, or the True Model Employer, or the Perfect Fabian Official, or the citizen of the Collectivist State. And it is best for us to see the full ugliness of the transformation which is passing over our Society in some such abrupt and even grotesque image at the end of it. The beginnings of a decline, in every age of history, have always had the appearance of being reforms. Nero not only fiddled while Rome was burning, but he probably really paid more attention to the fiddle than to the fire. The Roi Soleil, like many other soleils, was most splendid to all appearance a little before sunset. And if I ask myself what will be the ultimate and final fruit of all our social reforms, garden cities, model employers, insurances, exchanges, arbitration courts, and so on, then, I say, quite seriously, "I think it will be labour under the lash."

The Sultan and the Sack

Let us arrange in some order a number of converging considerations that all point in this direction. (1) It is broadly true, no doubt, that the weapon of the employer has hitherto been the threat of dismissal, that is, the threat of enforced starvation. He is a Sultan who need not order the bastinado, so long as he can order the sack. But there are not a few signs that this weapon is not quite so convenient and flexible a one as his increasing rapacities require. The fact of the introduction of fines, secretly or openly, in many shops and factories, proves that it is convenient for the capitalists to have some temporary and adjustable form of punishment besides the final punishment of pure ruin. Nor is it difficult to see the commonsense of this from their wholly inhuman point of view. The act of sacking a man is attended with the same disadvantages as the act of shooting a man: one of which is that you can get no more out of him. It is, I am told, distinctly annoying to blow a fellow creature's brains out with a revolver and then suddenly remember that he was the only person who knew where to get the best Russian cigarettes. So our Sultan, who is the orderer of the sack, is also the bearer of the bow-string. A school in which there was no punishment, except expulsion, would be a school in which it would be very difficult to keep proper discipline; and the sort of discipline on which the reformed capitalism will insist will be all of the type which in free nations is imposed only on children. Such a school would probably be in a chronic condition of breaking up for the holidays. And the reasons for the insufficiency of this extreme instrument are also varied and evident. The materialistic Sociologists, who talk about the survival of the fittest and the weakest going to the wall (and whose way of looking at the world is to put on the latest and most powerful scientific spectacles, and then shut their eyes), frequently talk as if a workman were simply efficient or non-efficient, as if a criminal were reclaimable or irreclaimable. The employers have sense enough at least to know better than that. They can see that a servant may be useful in one way and exasperating in another; that he may be bad in one part of his work and good in another; that he may be occasionally drunk and yet generally indispensable. Just as a practical school-master would know that a schoolboy can be at once the plague and the pride of the school. Under these circumstances small and varying penalties are obviously the most convenient things for the person keeping order; an underling can be punished for coming late, and yet do useful work when he comes. It will be possible to give a rap over the knuckles without wholly cutting off the right hand that has offended. Under these circumstances the employers have naturally resorted to fines. But there is a further ground for believing that the process will go beyond fines before it is completed.

(2) The fine is based on the old European idea that everybody possesses private property in some reasonable degree; but not only is this not true to-day, but it is not being made any truer, even by those who honestly believe that they are mending matters. The great employers will often do something towards improving what they call the "conditions" of their workers; but a worker might have his conditions as carefully arranged as a racehorse has, and still have no more personal property than a racehorse. If you take an average poor seamstress or factory girl, you will find that the power of chastising her through her property has very considerable limits; it is almost as hard for the employer of labour to tax her for punishment as it is for the Chancellor of the Exchequer to tax her for revenue. The next most obvious thing to think of, of course, would be imprisonment, and that might be effective enough under simpler conditions. An old-fashioned shopkeeper might have locked up his apprentice in his coal-cellar; but his coal-cellar would be a real, pitch dark coal-cellar, and the rest of his house would be a real human house. Everybody (especially the apprentice) would see a most perceptible difference between the two. But, as I pointed out in the article before this, the whole tendency of the capitalist legislation and experiment is to make imprisonment much more general and automatic, while making it, or professing to make it, more humane. In other words, the hygienic prison and the servile factory will become so uncommonly like each other that the poor man will hardly know or care whether he is at the moment expiating an offence or merely swelling a dividend. In both places there will be the same sort of shiny tiles. In neither place will there be any cell so unwholesome as a coal-cellar or so wholesome as a home. The weapon of the prison, therefore, like the weapon of the fine, will be found to have considerable limitations to its effectiveness when employed against the wretched reduced citizen of our day. Whether it be property or liberty you cannot take from him what he has not got. You cannot imprison a slave, because you cannot enslave a slave.

The Barbarous Revival

(3) Most people, on hearing the suggestion that it may come to corporal punishment at last (as it did in every slave system I ever heard of, including some that were generally kindly, and even successful), will merely be struck with horror and incredulity, and feel that such a barbarous revival is unthinkable in the modern atmosphere. How far it will be, or need be, a revival of the actual images and methods of ruder times I will discuss in a moment. But first, as another of the converging lines tending to corporal punishment, consider this: that for some reason or other the old full-blooded and masculine humanitarianism in this matter has weakened and fallen silent; it has weakened and fallen silent in a very curious manner, the precise reason for which I do not altogether understand. I knew the average Liberal, the average Nonconformist minister, the average Labour Member, the average middle-class Socialist, were, with all their good qualities, very deficient in what I consider a respect for the human soul. But I did imagine that they had the ordinary modern respect for the human body. The fact, however, is clear and incontrovertible. In spite of the horror of all humane people, in spite of the hesitation even of our corrupt and panic-stricken Parliament, measures can now be triumphantly passed for spreading or increasing the use of physical torture, and for applying it to the newest and vaguest categories of crime. Thirty or forty years ago, nay, twenty years ago, when Mr. F. Hugh O'Donnell and others forced a Liberal Government to drop the cat-o-nine-tails like a scorpion, we could have counted on a mass of honest hatred of such things. We cannot count on it now.

(4) But lastly, it is not necessary that in the factories of the future the institution of physical punishment should actually remind people of the jambok or the knout. It could easily be developed out of the many forms of physical discipline which are already used by employers on the excuses of education or hygiene. Already in some factories girls are obliged to swim whether they like it or not, or do gymnastics whether they like it or not. By a simple extension of hours or complication of exercises a pair of Swedish clubs could easily be so used as to leave their victim as exhausted as one who had come off the rack. I think it extremely likely that they will be.

IX. THE MASK OF SOCIALISM

The chief aim of all honest Socialists just now is to prevent the coming of Socialism. I do not say it as a sneer, but, on the contrary, as a compliment; a compliment to their political instinct and public spirit. I admit it may be called an exaggeration; but there really is a sort of sham Socialism that the modern politicians may quite possibly agree to set up; if they do succeed in setting it up, the battle for the poor is lost.

We must note, first of all, a general truth about the curious time we live in. It will not be so difficult as some people may suppose to make the Servile State look rather like Socialism, especially to the more pedantic kind of Socialist. The reason is this. The old lucid and trenchant expounder of Socialism, such as Blatchford or Fred Henderson, always describes the economic power of the plutocrats as consisting in private property. Of course, in a sense, this is quite true; though they too often miss the point that private property, as such, is not the same as property confined to the few. But the truth is that the situation has grown much more subtle; perhaps too subtle, not to say too insane, for straight-thinking theorists like Blatchford. The rich man to-day does not only rule by using private property; he also rules by treating public property as if it were private property. A man like Lord Murray pulled the strings, especially the purse-strings; but the whole point of his position was that all sorts of strings had got entangled. The secret strength of the money he held did not lie merely in the fact that it was his money. It lay precisely in the fact that nobody had any clear idea of whether it was his money, or his successor's money, or his brother's money, or the Marconi Company's money, or the Liberal Party's money, or the English Nation's money. It was buried treasure; but it was not private property. It was the acme of plutocracy because it was not private property. Now, by following this precedent, this unprincipled vagueness about official and unofficial moneys by the cheerful habit of always mixing up the money in the pocket with the money in the till, it would be quite possible to keep the rich as rich as ever in practice, though they might have suffered confiscation in theory. Mr. Lloyd George has four hundred a year as an M. P.; but he not only gets much more as a Minister, but he might at any time get immeasurably more by speculating on State secrets that are necessarily known to him. Some say that he has even attempted something of the kind. Now, it would be quite possible to cut Mr. George down, not to four hundred a year, but to fourpence a day; and still leave him all these other and enormous financial superiorities. It must be remembered that a Socialist State, in any way resembling a modern State, must, however egalitarian it may be, have the handling of huge sums, and the enjoyment of large conveniences; it is not improbable that the same men will handle and enjoy in much the same manner, though in theory they are doing it as instruments, and not as individuals. For instance, the Prime Minister has a private house, which is also (I grieve to inform that eminent Puritan) a public house. It is supposed to be a sort of Government office; though people do not generally give children's parties, or go to bed in a Government office. I do not know where Mr. Herbert Samuel lives; but I have no doubt he does himself well in the matter of decoration and furniture. On the existing official parallel there is no need to move any of these things in order to Socialise them. There is no need to withdraw one diamond-headed nail from the carpet; or one golden teaspoon from the tray. It is only necessary to call it an official residence, like 10 Downing-street. I think it is not at all improbable that this Plutocracy, pretending to be a Bureaucracy, will be attempted or achieved. Our wealthy rulers will be in the position which grumblers in the world of sport sometimes attribute to some of the "gentlemen" players. They assert that some of these are paid like any professional; only their pay is called their expenses. This system might run side by side with a theory of equal wages, as absolute as that once laid down by Mr. Bernard Shaw. By the theory of the State, Mr. Herbert Samuel and Mr. Lloyd George might be humble citizens, drudging for their fourpence a day; and no better off than porters and coal-heavers. If there were presented to our mere senses what appeared to be the form of Mr. Herbert Samuel in an astrakhan coat and a motor-car, we should find the record of the expenditure (if we could find it at all) under the heading of "Speed Limit Extension Enquiry Commission." If it fell to our lot to behold (with the eye of flesh) what seemed to be Mr. Lloyd George lying in a hammock and smoking a costly cigar, we should know that the expenditure would be divided between the "Condition of Rope and Netting Investigation Department," and the "State of Cuban Tobacco Trade: Imperial Inspector's Report."

Such is the society I think they will build unless we can knock it down as fast as they build it. Everything in it, tolerable or intolerable, will have but one use; and that use what our ancestors used to call usance or usury. Its art may be good or bad, but it will be an advertisement for usurers; its literature may be good or bad, but it will appeal to the patronage of usurers; its scientific selection will select according to the needs of usurers; its religion will be just charitable enough to pardon usurers; its penal system will be just cruel enough to crush all the critics of usurers: the truth of it will be Slavery: and the title of it may quite possibly be Socialism.

THE ESCAPE

We watched you building, stone by stone,
The well-washed cells and well-washed graves
We shall inhabit but not own
When Britons ever shall be slaves;
The water's waiting in the trough,
The tame oats sown are portioned free,
There is Enough, and just Enough,
And all is ready now but we.
But you have not caught us yet, my lords,
You have us still to get.
A sorry army you'd have got,
Its flags are rags that float and rot,
Its drums are empty pan and pot,
Its baggage is—an empty cot;
But you have not caught us yet.
A little; and we might have slipped
When came your rumours and your sales
And the foiled rich men, feeble-lipped,
Said and unsaid their sorry tales;
Great God! It needs a bolder brow
To keep ten sheep inside a pen,
And we are sheep no longer now;
You are but Masters. We are Men.
We give you all good thanks, my lords,
We buy at easy price;
Thanks for the thousands that you stole,
The bribes by wire, the bets on coal,
The knowledge of that naked whole
That hath delivered our flesh and soul
Out of your Paradise.
We had held safe your parks; but when
Men taunted you with bribe and fee,
We only saw the Lord of Men
Grin like an Ape and climb a tree;
And humbly had we stood without
Your princely barns; did we not see
In pointed faces peering out
What Rats now own the granary.

It is too late, too late, my lords,
We give you back your grace:
You cannot with all cajoling
Make the wet ditch, or winds that sting,
Lost pride, or the pawned wedding rings,
Or drink or Death a blacker thing
Than a smile upon your face.

THE NEW RAID

The two kinds of social reform, one of which might conceivably free us at last while the other would certainly enslave us forever, are exhibited in an easy working model in the two efforts that have been made for the soldiers' wives—I mean the effort to increase their allowance and the effort to curtail their alleged drinking. In the preliminary consideration, at any rate, we must see the second question as quite detached from our own sympathies on the special subject of fermented liquor. It could be applied to any other pleasure or ornament of life; it will be applied to every other pleasure and ornament of life if the Capitalist campaign can succeed. The argument we know; but it cannot be too often made clear. An employer, let us say, pays a seamstress twopence a day, and she does not seem to thrive on it. So little, perhaps, does she thrive on it that the employer has even some difficulty in thriving upon her. There are only two things that he can do, and the distinction between them cuts the whole social and political world in two. It is a touchstone by which we can—not sometimes, but always—distinguish economic equality from servile social reform. He can give the girl some magnificent sum, such as sixpence a day, to do as she likes with, and trust that her improved health and temper will work for the benefit of his business. Or he may keep her to the original sum of a shilling a week, but earmark each of the pennies to be used or not to be used for a particular purpose. If she must not spend this penny on a bunch of violets, or that penny on a novelette, or the other penny on a toy for some baby, it is possible that she will concentrate her expenditure more upon physical necessities, and so become, from the employer's point of view, a more efficient person. Without the trouble of adding twopence to her wages, he has added twopenny-worth to her food. In short, she has the holy satisfaction of being worth more without being paid more.

This Capitalist is an ingenious person, and has many polished characteristics; but I think the most singular thing about him is his staggering lack of shame. Neither the hour of death nor the day of reckoning, neither the tent of exile nor the house of mourning, neither chivalry nor patriotism, neither womanhood nor widowhood, is safe at this supreme moment from his dirty little expedient of dieting the slave. As similar bullies, when they collect the slum rents, put a foot in the open door, these are always ready to push in a muddy wedge wherever there is a slit in a sundered household or a crack in a broken heart. To a man of any manhood nothing can be conceived more loathsome and sacrilegious than even so much as asking whether a woman who has given up all she loved to death and the fatherland has or has not shown some weakness in her seeking for self-comfort. I know not in which of the two cases I should count myself the baser for inquiring—a case where the charge was false or a case where it was true. But the philanthropic employer of the sort I describe is not a man of any manhood; in a sense he is not a man at all. He shows some consciousness of the fact when he calls his workers "men" as distinct from masters. He cannot comprehend the gallantry of costermongers or the delicacy that is quite common among cabmen. He finds this social reform by half-rations on the whole to his mercantile profit, and it will be hard to get him to think of anything else.

But there are people assisting him, people like the Duchess of Marlborough, who know not their right hand from their left, and to these we may legitimately address our remonstrance and a resume of some of the facts they do not know. The Duchess of Marlborough is, I believe, an American, and this separates her from the problem in a special way, because the drink question in America is entirely different from the drink question in England. But I wish the Duchess of Marlborough would pin up in her private study, side by side with the Declaration of Independence, a document recording the following simple truths: (1) Beer, which is largely drunk in public-houses, is not a spirit or a grog or a cocktail or a drug. It is the common English liquid for quenching the thirst; it is so still among innumerable gentlemen, and, until very lately, was so among innumerable ladies. Most of us remember dames of the last generation whose manners were fit for Versailles, and who drank ale or Stout as a matter of course. Schoolboys drank ale as a matter of course, and their schoolmasters gave it to them as a matter of course. To tell a poor woman that she must not have any until half the day is over is simply cracked, like telling a dog or a child that he must not have water. (2) The public-house is not a secret rendezvous of bad characters. It is the open and obvious place for a certain purpose, which all men used for that purpose until the rich began to be snobs and the poor to become slaves. One might as well warn people against Willesden Junction. (3) Many poor people live in houses where they cannot, without great preparation, offer hospitality. (4) The climate of these picturesque islands does not favour conducting long conversations with one's oldest friends on an iron seat in the park. (5) Halfpast eleven a.m. is not early in the day for a woman who gets up before six. (6) The bodies and minds of these women belong to God and to themselves.

THE NEW NAME

Something has come into our community, which is strong enough to save our community; but which has not yet got a name. Let no one fancy I confess any unreality when I confess the namelessness. The morality called Puritanism, the tendency called Liberalism, the reaction called Tory Democracy, had not only long been powerful, but had practically done most of their work, before these actual names were attached to them. Nevertheless, I think it would be a good thing to have some portable and practicable way of referring to those who think as we do in our main concern. Which is, that men in England are ruled, at this minute by the clock, by brutes who refuse them bread, by liars who refuse them news, and by fools who cannot govern, and therefore wish to enslave.

Let me explain first why I am not satisfied with the word commonly used, which I have often used myself; and which, in some contexts, is quite the right word to use. I mean the word "rebel." Passing over the fact that many who understand the justice of our cause (as a great many at the Universities) would still use the word "rebel" in its old and strict sense as meaning only a disturber of just rule. I pass to a much more practical point. The word "rebel" understates our cause. It is much too mild; it lets our enemies off much too easily. There is a tradition in all western life and letters of Prometheus defying the stars, of man at war with the Universe, and dreaming what nature had never dared to dream. All this is valuable in its place and proportion. But it has nothing whatever to do with our ease; or rather it very much weakens it. The plutocrats will be only too pleased if we profess to preach a new morality; for they know jolly well that they have broken the old one. They will be only too pleased to be able to say that we, by our own confession, are merely restless and negative; that we are only what we call rebels and they call cranks. But it is not true; and we must not concede it to them for a moment. The model millionaire is more of a crank than the Socialists; just as Nero was more of a crank than the Christians. And avarice has gone mad in the governing class to-day, just as lust went mad in the circle of Nero. By all the working and orthodox standards of sanity, capitalism is insane. I should not say to Mr. Rockefeller "I am a rebel." I should say "I am a respectable man: and you are not."

Our Lawless Enemies

But the vital point is that the confession of mere rebellion softens the startling lawlessness of our enemies. Suppose a publisher's clerk politely asked his employer for a rise in his salary; and, on being refused, said he must leave the employment? Suppose the employer knocked him down with a ruler, tied him up as a brown paper parcel, addressed him (in a fine business hand) to the Governor of Rio Janeiro and then asked the policeman to promise never to arrest him for what he had done? That is a precise copy, in every legal and moral principle, of the "deportation of the strikers." They were assaulted and kidnapped for not accepting a contract, and for nothing else; and the act was so avowedly criminal that the law had to be altered afterwards to cover the crime. Now suppose some postal official, between here and Rio Janeiro, had noticed a faint kicking inside the brown paper parcel, and had attempted to ascertain the cause. And suppose the clerk could only explain, in a muffled voice through the brown paper, that he was by constitution and temperament a Rebel. Don't you see that he would be rather understating his case? Don't you see he would be bearing his injuries much too meekly? They might take him out of the parcel; but they would very possibly put him into a mad-house instead. Symbolically speaking, that is what they would like to do with us. Symbolically speaking, the dirty misers who rule us will put us in a mad-house—unless we can put them there.

Or suppose a bank cashier were admittedly allowed to take the money out of the till, and put it loose in his pocket, more or less mixed up with his own money; afterwards laying some of both (at different odds) on "Blue Murder" for the Derby. Suppose when some depositor asked mildly what day the accountants came, he smote that astonished inquirer on the nose, crying: "Slanderer! Mud-slinger!" and suppose he then resigned his position. Suppose no books were shown. Suppose when the new cashier came to be initiated into his duties, the old cashier did not tell him about the money, but confided it to the honour and delicacy of his own maiden aunt at Cricklewood. Suppose he then went off in a yacht to visit the whale fisheries of the North Sea. Well, in every moral and legal principle, that is a precise account of the dealings with the Party Funds. But what would the banker say? What would the clients say? One thing, I think, I can venture to promise; the banker would not march up and down the office exclaiming in rapture, "I'm a rebel! That's what I am, a rebel!" And if he said to the first indignant depositor "You are a rebel," I fear the depositor might answer, "You are a robber." We have no need to elaborate arguments for breaking the law. The capitalists have broken the law. We have no need of further moralities. They have broken their own morality. It is as if you were to run down the street shouting, "Communism! Communism! Share! Share!" after a man who had run away with your watch.

We want a term that will tell everybody that there is, by the common standard, frank fraud and cruelty pushed to their fierce extreme; and that we are fighting THEM. We are not in a state of "divine discontent"; we are in an entirely human and entirely reasonable rage. We say we have been swindled and oppressed, and we are quite ready and able to prove it before any tribunal that allows us to call a swindler a swindler. It is the protection of the present system that most of its tribunals do not. I cannot at the moment think of any party name that would particularly distinguish us from our more powerful and prosperous opponents, unless it were the name the old Jacobites gave themselves; the Honest Party.

Captured Our Standards

I think it is plain that for the purpose of facing these new and infamous modern facts, we cannot, with any safety, depend on any of the old nineteenth century names; Socialist, or Communist, or Radical, or Liberal, or Labour. They are all honourable names; they all stand, or stood, for things in which we may still believe; we can still apply them to other problems; but not to this one. We have no longer a monopoly of these names. Let it be understood that I am not speaking here of the philosophical problem of their meaning, but of the practical problem of their use. When I called myself a Radical I knew Mr. Balfour would not call himself a Radical; therefore there was some use in the word. When I called myself a Socialist I knew Lord Penrhyn would not call himself a Socialist; therefore there was some use in the word. But the capitalists, in that aggressive march which is the main fact of our time, have captured our standards, both in the military and philosophic sense of the word. And it is useless for us to march under colours which they can carry as well as we.

Do you believe in Democracy? The devils also believe and tremble. Do you believe in Trades Unionism? The Labour Members also believe; and tremble like a falling teetotum. Do you believe in the State? The Samuels also believe, and grin. Do you believe in the centralisation of Empire? So did Beit. Do you believe in the decentralisation of Empire? So does Albu. Do you believe in the brotherhood of men: and do you, dear brethren, believe that Brother Arthur Henderson does not? Do you cry, "The world for the workers!" and do you imagine Philip Snowden would not? What we need is a name that shall declare, not that the modern treason and tyranny are bad, but that they are quite literally, intolerable: and that we mean to act accordingly. I really think "the Limits" would be as good a name as any. But, anyhow, something is born among us that is as strong as an infant Hercules: and it is part of my prejudices to want it christened. I advertise for godfathers and godmothers.

A WORKMAN'S HISTORY OF ENGLAND

A thing which does not exist and which is very much wanted is "A Working-Man's History of England." I do not mean a history written for working men (there are whole dustbins of them), I mean a history, written by working men or from the working men's standpoint. I wish five generations of a fisher's or a miner's family could incarnate themselves in one man and tell the story.

It is impossible to ignore altogether any comment coming from so eminent a literary artist as Mr. Laurence Housman, but I do not deal here so specially with his well known conviction about Votes for Women, as with another idea which is, I think, rather at the back of it, if not with him at least with others; and which concerns this matter of the true story of England. For the true story is so entirely different from the false official story that the official classes tell that by this time the working class itself has largely forgotten its own experience. Either story can be quite logically linked up with Female Suffrage, which, therefore, I leave where it is for the moment; merely confessing that, so long as we get hold of the right story and not the wrong story, it seems to me a matter of secondary importance whether we link it up with Female Suffrage or not.

Now the ordinary version of recent English history that most moderately educated people have absorbed from childhood is something like this. That we emerged slowly from a semi-barbarism in which all the power and wealth were in the hands of Kings and a few nobles; that the King's power was broken first and then in due time that of the nobles, that this piece-meal improvement was brought about by one class after another waking up to a sense of citizenship and demanding a place in the national councils, frequently by riot or violence; and that in consequence of such menacing popular action, the franchise was granted to one class after another and used more and more to improve the social conditions of those classes, until we practically became a democracy, save for such exceptions as that of the women. I do not think anyone will deny that something like that is the general idea of the educated man who reads a newspaper and of the newspaper that he reads. That is the view current at public schools and colleges; it is part of the culture of all the classes that count for much in government; and there is not one word of truth in it from beginning to end.

That Great Reform Bill

Wealth and political power were very much more popularly distributed in the Middle Ages than they are now; but we will pass all that and consider recent history. The franchise has never been largely and liberally granted in England; half the males have no vote and are not likely to get one. It was *never* granted in reply to pressure from awakened sections of the democracy; in every case there was a perfectly clear motive for granting it solely for the convenience of the aristocrats. The Great Reform Bill was not passed in response to such riots as that which destroyed a Castle; nor did the men who destroyed the Castle get any advantage whatever out of the Great Reform Bill. The Great Reform Bill was passed in order to seal an alliance between the landed aristocrats and the rich manufacturers of the north (an alliance that rules us still); and the chief object of that alliance was to *prevent* the English populace getting any political power in the general excitement after the French Revolution. No one can read Macaulay's speech on the Chartists, for instance, and not see that this is so. Disraeli's further extension of the suffrage was not effected by the intellectual vivacity and pure republican theory of the mid-Victorian agricultural labourer; it was effected by a politician who saw an opportunity to dish the Whigs, and guessed that certain orthodoxies in the more prosperous artisan might yet give him a balance against the commercial Radicals. And while this very thin game of wire-pulling with the mere abstraction of the vote was being worked entirely by the oligarchs and entirely in their interests, the solid and real thing that was going on was the steady despoiling of the poor of all power or wealth, until they find themselves to-day upon the threshold of slavery. That is The Working Man's History of England.

Now, as I have said, I care comparatively little what is done with the mere voting part of the matter, so long as it is not claimed in such a way as to allow the plutocrat to escape his responsibility for his crimes, by pretending to be much more progressive, or much more susceptible to popular protest, than he ever has been. And there is this danger in many of those who have answered me. One of them, for instance, says that women have been forced into their present industrial situations by the same iron economic laws that have compelled men. I say that men have not been compelled by iron economic laws, but in the main by the coarse and Christless cynicism of other men. But, of course, this way of talking is exactly in accordance with the fashionable and official version of English history. Thus, you will read that the monasteries, places where men of the poorest origin could be powerful, grew corrupt and gradually decayed. Or you will read that the mediaeval guilds of free workmen yielded at last to an inevitable economic law. You will read this; and you will be reading lies. They might as well say that Julius Caesar gradually decayed at the foot of Pompey's statue. You might as well say that Abraham Lincoln yielded at last to an inevitable economic law. The free mediaeval guilds did not decay; they were murdered. Solid men with solid guns and halberds, armed with lawful warrants from living statesmen broke up their corporations and took away their hard cash from them. In the same way the people in Cradley Heath are no more victims of a necessary economic law than the people in Putumayo. They are victims of a very terrible creature, of whose sins much has been said since the beginning of the world; and of whom it was said of old, "Let us fall into the hands of God, for His mercies are great; but let us not fall into the hands of Man."

The Capitalist Is in the Dock

Now it is this offering of a false economic excuse for the sweater that is the danger in perpetually saying that the poor woman will use the vote and that the poor man has not used it. The poor man is prevented from using it; prevented by the rich man, and the poor woman would be prevented in exactly the same gross and stringent style. I do not deny, of course, that there is something in the English temperament, and in the heritage of the last few centuries that makes the English workman more tolerant of wrong than most foreign workmen would be. But this only slightly modifies the main fact of the moral responsibility. To take an imperfect parallel, if we said that negro slaves would have rebelled if negroes had been more intelligent, we should be saying what is reasonable. But if we were to say that it could by any possibility be represented as being the negro's fault that he was at that moment in America and not in Africa, we should be saying what is frankly unreasonable. It is every bit as unreasonable to say the mere supineness of the English workmen has put them in the capitalist slave-yard. The capitalist has put them in the capitalist slaveyard; and very cunning smiths have hammered the chains. It is just this creative criminality in the authors of the system that we must not allow to be slurred over. The capitalist is in the dock to-day; and so far as I at least can prevent him, he shall not get out of it.

THE FRENCH REVOLUTION AND THE IRISH

It will be long before the poison of the Party System is worked out of the body politic. Some of its most indirect effects are the most dangerous. One that is very dangerous just now is this: that for most Englishmen the Party System falsifies history, and especially the history of revolutions. It falsifies history because it simplifies history. It paints everything either Blue or Buff in the style of its own silly circus politics: while a real revolution has as many colours as the sunrise—or the end of the world. And if we do not get rid of this error we shall make very bad blunders about the real revolution which seems to grow more and more probable, especially among the Irish. And any human familiarity with history will teach a man this first of all: that Party practically does not exist in a real revolution. It is a game for quiet times.

If you take a boy who has been to one of those big private schools which are falsely called the Public Schools, and another boy who has been to one of those large public schools which are falsely called the Board Schools, you will find some differences between the two, chiefly a difference in the management of the voice. But you will find they are both English in a special way, and that their education has been essentially the same. They are ignorant on the same subjects. They have never heard of the same plain facts. They have been taught the wrong answer to the same confusing question. There is one fundamental element in the attitude of the Eton master talking about "playing the game," and the elementary teacher training gutter-snipes to sing, "What is the Meaning of Empire Day?" And the name of that element is "unhistoric." It knows nothing really about England, still less about Ireland or France, and, least of all, of course, about anything like the French Revolution.

Revolution by Snap Division
Now what general notion does the ordinary English boy, thus taught to utter one ignorance in one of two accents, get and keep through life about the French Revolution? It is the notion of the English House of Commons with an enormous Radical majority

on one side of the table and a small Tory minority on the other; the majority voting solid for a Republic, the minority voting solid for a Monarchy; two teams tramping through two lobbies with no difference between their methods and ours, except that (owing to some habit peculiar to Gaul) the brief intervals were brightened by a riot or a massacre, instead of by a whisky and soda and a Marconi tip. Novels are much more reliable than histories in such matters. For though an English novel about France does not tell the truth about France, it does tell the truth about England; and more than half the histories never tell the truth about anything. And popular fiction, I think, bears witness to the general English impression. The French Revolution is a snap division with an unusual turnover of votes. On the one side stand a king and queen who are good but weak, surrounded by nobles with rapiers drawn; some of whom are good, many of whom are wicked, all of whom are good-looking. Against these there is a formless mob of human beings, wearing red caps and seemingly insane, who all blindly follow ruffians who are also rhetoricians; some of whom die repentant and others unrepentant towards the end of the fourth act. The leaders of this boiling mass of all men melted into one are called Mirabeau, Robespierre, Danton, Marat, and so on. And it is conceded that their united frenzy may have been forced on them by the evils of the old regime.

That, I think, is the commonest English view of the French Revolution; and it will not survive the reading of two pages of any real speech or letter of the period. These human beings were human; varied, complex and inconsistent. But the rich Englishman, ignorant of revolutions, would hardly believe you if you told him some of the common human subtleties of the case. Tell him that Robespierre threw the red cap in the dirt in disgust, while the king had worn it with a broad grin, so to speak; tell him that Danton, the fierce founder of the Republic of the Terror, said quite sincerely to a noble, "I am more monarchist than you;" tell him that the Terror really seems to have been brought to an end chiefly by the efforts of people who particularly wanted to go on with it—and he will not believe these things. He will not believe them because he has no humility, and therefore no realism. He has never been inside himself; and so could never be inside another man. The truth is that in the French affair everybody occupied an individual position. Every man talked sincerely, if not because he was sincere, then because he was angry. Robespierre talked even more about God than about the Republic because he cared even more about God than about the Republic. Danton talked even more about France than about the Republic because he cared even more about France than about the Republic. Marat talked more about Humanity than either, because that physician (though himself somewhat needing a physician) really cared about it. The nobles were divided, each man from the next. The attitude of the king was quite different from the attitude of the queen; certainly much more different than any differences between our Liberals and Tories for the last twenty years. And it will sadden *some* of my friends to remember that it was the king who was the Liberal and the queen who was the Tory. There were not two people, I think, in that most practical crisis who stood in precisely the same attitude towards the situation. And that is why, between them, they saved Europe. It is when you really perceive the unity of mankind that you really perceive its variety. It is not a flippancy, it is a very sacred truth, to say that when men really understand that they are brothers they instantly begin to fight.

The Revival of Reality

Now these things are repeating themselves with an enormous reality in the Irish Revolution. You will not be able to make a Party System out of the matter. Everybody is in revolt; therefore everybody is telling the truth. The Nationalists will go on caring most for the nation, as Danton and the defenders of the frontier went on caring most for the nation. The priests will go on caring most for religion, as Robespierre went on caring most for religion. The Socialists will go on caring most for the cure of physical suffering, as Marat went on caring most for it. It is out of these real differences that real things can be made, such as the modern French democracy. For by such tenacity everyone sees at last that there is something in the other person's position. And those drilled in party discipline see nothing either past or present. And where there is nothing there is Satan.

For a long time past in our politics there has not only been no real battle, but no real bargain. No two men have bargained as Gladstone and Parnell bargained—each knowing the other to be a power. But in real revolutions men discover that no one man can really agree with another man until he has disagreed with him.

LIBERALISM: A SAMPLE

There is a certain daily paper in England towards which I feel very much as Tom Pinch felt towards Mr. Pecksniff immediately after he had found him out. The war upon Dickens was part of the general war on all democrats, about the eighties and nineties, which ushered in the brazen plutocracy of to-day. And one of the things that it was fashionable to say of Dickens in drawing-rooms was that he had no subtlety, and could not describe a complex frame of mind. Like most other things that are said in drawing-rooms, it was a lie. Dickens was a very unequal writer, and his successes alternate with his failures; but his successes are subtle quite as often as they are simple. Thus, to take "Martin Chuzzlewit" alone, I should call the joke about the Lord No-zoo a simple joke: but I should call the joke about Mrs. Todgers's vision of a wooden leg a subtle joke. And no frame of mind was ever so self-contradictory and yet so realistic as that which Dickens describes when he says, in effect, that, though Pinch knew now that there had never been such a person as Pecksniff, in his ideal sense, he could not bring himself to insult the very face and form that had contained the legend. The parallel with Liberal journalism is not perfect; because it was once honest; and Pecksniff presumably never was. And even when I come to feel a final incompatibility of temper, Pecksniff was not so Pecksniffian as he has since become. But the comparison is complete in so far as I share all the reluctance of Mr. Pinch. Some old heathen king was advised by one of the Celtic saints, I think, to burn what he had adored and adore what he had burnt. I am quite ready, if anyone will prove I was wrong, to adore what I have burnt; but I do really feel an unwillingness verging upon weakness to burning what I have adored. I think it is a weakness to be overcome in times as bad as these, when (as Mr. Orage wrote with something like splendid common sense the other day) there is such a lot to do and so few people who will do it. So I will devote this article to considering one case of the astounding baseness to which Liberal journalism has sunk.

Mental Breakdown in Fleet Street
One of the two or three streaks of light on our horizon can

be perceived in this: that the moral breakdown of these papers has been accompanied by a mental breakdown also. The contemporary official paper, like the "Daily News" or the "Daily Chronicle" (I mean in so far as it deals with politics), simply cannot argue; and simply does not pretend to argue. It considers the solution which it imagines that wealthy people want, and it signifies the same in the usual manner; which is not by holding up its hand, but by falling on its face. But there is no more curious quality in its degradation than a sort of carelessness, at once of hurry and fatigue, with which it flings down its argument—or rather its refusal to argue. It does not even write sophistry: it writes anything. It does not so much poison the reader's mind as simply assume that the reader hasn't got one. For instance, one of these papers printed an article on Sir Stuart Samuel, who, having broken the great Liberal statute against corruption, will actually, perhaps, be asked to pay his own fine—in spite of the fact that he can well afford to do so. The article says, if I remember aright, that the decision will cause general surprise and some indignation. That any modern Government making a very rich capitalist obey the law will cause general surprise, may be true. Whether it will cause general indignation rather depends on whether our social intercourse is entirely confined to Park Lane, or any such pigsties built of gold. But the journalist proceeds to say, his neck rising higher and higher out of his collar, and his hair rising higher and higher on his head, in short, his resemblance to the Dickens' original increasing every instant, that he does not mean that the law against corruption should be less stringent, but that the burden should be borne by the whole community. This may mean that whenever a rich man breaks the law, all the poor men ought to be made to pay his fine. But I will suppose a slightly less insane meaning. I will suppose it means that the whole power of the commonwealth should be used to prosecute an offender of this kind. That, of course, can only mean that the matter will be decided by that instrument which still pretends to represent the whole power of the commonwealth. In other words, the Government will judge the Government.

Now this is a perfectly plain piece of brute logic. We need not go into the other delicious things in the article, as when it says that "in old times Parliament had to be protected against Royal invasion by the man in the street." Parliament has to be protected now against the man in the street. Parliament is simply the most detested and the most detestable of all our national institutions: all that is evident enough. What is interesting is the blank and staring fallacy of the attempted reply.

When the Journalist Is Ruined

A long while ago, before all the Liberals died, a Liberal introduced a Bill to prevent Parliament being merely packed with the slaves of financial interests. For that purpose he established the excellent democratic principle that the private citizen, as such, might protest against public corruption. He was called the Common Informer. I believe the miserable party papers are really reduced to playing on the degradation of the two words in modern language. Now the word "common" in "Common Informer" means exactly what it means in "common sense" or "Book of Common Prayer," or (above all) in "House of Commons." It does not mean anything low or vulgar; any more than they do. The only difference is that the House of Commons really is low and vulgar; and the Common Informer isn't. It is just the same with the word "Informer." It does not mean spy or sneak. It means one who gives information. It means what "journalist" ought to mean. The only difference is that the Common Informer may be paid if he tells the truth. The common journalist will be ruined if he does.

Now the quite plain point before the party journalist is this: If he really means that a corrupt bargain between a Government and a contractor ought to be judged by public opinion, he must (nowadays) mean Parliament; that is, the caucus that controls Parliament. And he must decide between one of two views. Either he means that there can be no such thing as a corrupt Government. Or he means that it is one of the characteristic qualities of a corrupt Government to denounce its own corruption. I laugh; and I leave him his choice.

THE FATIGUE OF FLEET STREET

Why is the modern party political journalism so bad? It is worse even than it intends to be. It praises its preposterous party leaders through thick and thin; but it somehow succeeds in making them look greater fools than they are. This clumsiness clings even to the photographs of public men, as they are snapshotted at public meetings. A sensitive politician (if there is such a thing) would, I should think, want to murder the man who snapshots him at those moments. For our general impression of a man's gesture or play of feature is made up of a series of vanishing instants, at any one of which he may look worse than our general impression records. Mr. Augustine Birrell may have made quite a sensible and amusing speech, in the course of which his audience would hardly have noticed that he resettled his necktie. Snapshot him, and he appears as convulsively clutching his throat in the agonies of strangulation, and with his head twisted on one side as if he had been hanged. Sir Edward Carson might make a perfectly good speech, which no one thought wearisome, but might himself be just tired enough to shift from one leg to the other. Snapshot him, and he appears as holding one leg stiffly in the air and yawning enough to swallow the audience. But it is in the prose narratives of the Press that we find most manifestations of this strange ineptitude; this knack of exhibiting your own favourites in an unlucky light. It is not so much that the party journalists do not tell the truth as that they tell just enough of it to make it clear that they are telling lies. One of their favourite blunders is an amazing sort of bathos. They begin by telling you that some statesman said something brilliant in style or biting in wit, at which his hearers thrilled with terror or thundered with applause. And then they tell you what it was that he said. Silly asses!

Insane Exaggeration

Here is an example from a leading Liberal paper touching the debates on Home Rule. I am a Home Ruler; so my sympathies would be, if anything, on the side of the Liberal paper upon that point. I merely quote it as an example of this ridiculous way of writing, which, by insane exaggeration, actually makes its hero look smaller than he is.

This was strange language to use about the "hypocritical sham," and Mr. Asquith, knowing that the biggest battle of his career was upon him, hit back without mercy. "I should like first to know," said he, with a glance at his supporters, "whether my proposals are accepted?"

That's all. And I really do not see why poor Mr. Asquith should be represented as having violated the Christian virtue of mercy by saying that. I myself could compose a great many paragraphs upon the same model, each containing its stinging and perhaps unscrupulous epigram. As, for example:—"The Archbishop of Canterbury, realising that his choice now lay between denying God and earning the crown of martyrdom by dying in torments, spoke with a frenzy of religious passion that might have seemed fanatical under circumstances less intense. 'The Children's Service,' he said firmly, with his face to the congregation, 'will be held at half-past four this afternoon as usual.'"

Or, we might have:—"Lord Roberts, recognising that he had now to face Armageddon, and that if he lost this last battle against overwhelming odds the independence of England would be extinguished forever, addressed to his soldiers (looking at them and not falling off his horse) a speech which brought their national passions to boiling point, and might well have seemed blood-thirsty in quieter times. It ended with the celebrated declaration that it was a fine day."

Or we might have the much greater excitement of reading something like this:—"The Astronomer Royal, having realised that the earth would certainly be smashed to pieces by a comet unless his requests in connection with wireless telegraphy were seriously considered, gave an address at the Royal Society which, under other circumstances, would have seemed unduly dogmatic and emotional and deficient in scientific agnosticism. This address (which he delivered without any attempt to stand on his head) included a fierce and even ferocious declaration that it is generally easier to see the stars by night than by day."

Now, I cannot see, on my conscience and reason, that any one of my imaginary paragraphs is more ridiculous than the real one. Nobody can believe that Mr. Asquith regards these belated and careful compromises about Home Rule as "the biggest battle of his career." It is only justice to him to say that he has had bigger battles than that. Nobody can believe that any body of men, bodily present, either thundered or thrilled at a man merely saying that he would like to know whether his proposals were accepted. No; it would be far better for Parliament if its doors were shut again, and reporters were excluded. In that case, the outer public did hear genuine rumours of almost gigantic eloquence; such as that which has perpetuated Pitt's reply against the charge of youth, or Fox's bludgeoning of the idea of war as a compromise. It would be much better to follow the old fashion and let in no reporters at all than to follow the new fashion and select the stupidest reporters you can find.

Their Load of Lies

Now, why do people in Fleet-street talk such tosh? People in Fleet-street are not fools. Most of them have realised reality through work; some through starvation; some through damnation, or something damnably like it. I think it is simply and seriously true that they are tired of their job. As the general said in M. Rostand's play, "la fatigue!"

I do really believe that this is one of the ways in which God (don't get flurried, Nature if you like) is unexpectedly avenged on things infamous and unreasonable. And this method is that men's moral and even physical tenacity actually give out under such a load of lies. They go on writing their leading articles and their Parliamentary reports. They go on doing it as a convict goes on picking oakum. But the point is not that we are bored with their articles; the point is that they are. The work is done worse because it is done weakly and without human enthusiasm. And it is done weakly because of the truth we have told so many times in this book: that it is not done for monarchy, for which men will die; or for democracy, for which men will die; or even for aristocracy, for which many men have died. It is done for a thing called Capitalism: which stands out quite clearly in history in many curious ways. But the most curious thing about it is that no man has loved it; and no man died for it.

THE AMNESTY FOR AGGRESSION

If there is to rise out of all this red ruin something like a republic of justice, it is essential that our views should be real views; that is, glimpses of lives and landscapes outside ourselves. It is essential that they should not be mere opium visions that begin and end in smoke—and so often in cannon smoke. I make no apology, therefore, for returning to the purely practical and realistic point I urged last week: the fact that we shall lose everything we might have gained if we lose the idea that the responsible person is responsible.

For instance, it is almost specially so with the one or two things in which the British Government, or the British public, really are behaving badly. The first, and worst of them, is the non-extension of the Moratorium, or truce of debtor and creditor, to the very world where there are the poorest debtors and the cruellest creditors. This is infamous: and should be, if possible, more infamous to those who think the war right than to those who think it wrong. Everyone knows that the people who can least pay their debts are the people who are always trying to. Among the poor a payment may be as rash as a speculation. Among the rich a bankruptcy may be as safe as a bank. Considering the class from which private soldiers are taken, there is an atrocious meanness in the idea of buying their blood abroad, while we sell their sticks at home. The English language, by the way, is full of delicate paradoxes. We talk of the private soldiers because they are really public soldiers; and we talk of the public schools because they are really private schools. Anyhow, the wrong is of the sort that ought to be resisted, as much in war as in peace.

Ought to Be Hammered

But as long as we speak of it as a cloudy conclusion, come to by an anonymous club called Parliament, or a masked tribunal called the Cabinet, we shall never get such a wrong righted. Somebody is officially responsible for the unfairness; and that somebody ought to be hammered. The other example, less important but more ludicrous, is the silly boycott of Germans in England, extending even to German music. I do not believe for a moment that the English people feel any such insane fastidiousness. Are the English artists who practise the particularly English art of water-colour to be forbidden to use Prussian blue? Are all old ladies to shoot their Pomeranian dogs? But though England would laugh at this, she will get the credit of it, and will continue: until we ask who the actual persons are who feel sure that we should shudder at a ballad of the Rhine. It is certain that we should find they are capitalists. It is very probable that we should find they are foreigners.

Some days ago the Official Council of the Independent Labour Party, or the Independent Council of the Official Labour Party, or the Independent and Official Council of the Labour Party (I have got quite nervous about these names and distinctions; but they all seem to say the same thing) began their manifesto by saying it would be difficult to assign the degrees of responsibility which each nation had for the outbreak of the war. Afterwards, a writer in the "Christian Commonwealth," lamenting war in the name of Labour, but in the language of my own romantic middle-class, said that all the nations must share the responsibility for this great calamity of war. Now exactly as long as we go on talking like that we shall have war after war, and calamity after calamity, until the crack of doom. It simply amounts to a promise of pardon to any person who will start a quarrel. It is an amnesty for assassins. The moment any man assaults any other man he makes all the other men as bad as himself. He has only to stab, and to vanish in a fog of forgetfulness. The real eagles of iron, the predatory Empires, will be delighted with this doctrine. They will applaud the Labour Concert or Committee, or whatever it is called. They will willingly take all the crime, with only a quarter of the conscience: they will be as ready to share the memory as they are to share the spoil. The Powers will divide responsibility as calmly as they divided Poland.

The Whole Loathsome Load

But I still stubbornly and meekly submit my point: that you cannot end war without asking who began it. If you think somebody else, not Germany, began it, then blame that somebody else: do not blame everybody and nobody. Perhaps you think that a small sovereign people, fresh from two triumphant wars, ought to discrown itself before sunrise;

because the nephew of a neighbouring Emperor has been shot by his own subjects. Very well. Then blame Servia; and, to the extent of your influence, you may be preventing small kingdoms being obstinate or even princes being shot. Perhaps you think the whole thing was a huge conspiracy of Russia, with France as a dupe and Servia as a pretext. Very well. Then blame Russia; and, to the extent of your influence, you may be preventing great Empires from making racial excuses for a raid. Perhaps you think France wrong for feeling what you call "revenge," and I should call recovery of stolen goods. Perhaps you blame Belgium for being sentimental about her frontier; or England for being sentimental about her word. If so, blame them; or whichever of them you think is to blame. Or again, it is barely possible that you may think, as I do, that the whole loathsome load has been laid upon us by the monarchy which I have not named; still less wasted time in abusing. But if there be in Europe a military State which has not the religion of Russia, yet has helped Russia to tyrannise over the Poles, that State cares not for religion, but for tyranny. If there be a State in Europe which has not the religion of the Austrians, but has helped Austria to bully the Servians, that State cares not for belief, but for bullying. If there be in Europe any people or principality which respects neither republics nor religions, to which the political ideal of Paris is as much a myth as the mystical ideal of Moscow, then blame that: and do more than blame. In the healthy and highly theological words of Robert Blatchford, drive it back to the Hell from which it came.

Crying Over Spilt Blood

But whatever you do, do not blame everybody for what was certainly done by somebody. It may be it is no good crying over spilt blood, any more than over spilt milk. But we do not find the culprit any more by spilling the milk over everybody; or by daubing everybody with blood. Still less do we improve matters by watering the milk with our tears, nor the blood either. To say that everybody is responsible means that nobody is responsible. If in the future we see Russia annexing Rutland (as part of the old Kingdom of Muscovy), if we see Bavaria taking a sudden fancy to the Bank of England, or the King of the Cannibal Islands suddenly demanding a tribute of edible boys and girls from England and America, we may be quite certain also that the Leader of the Labour Party will rise, with a slight cough, and say: "It would be a difficult task to apportion the blame between the various claims which..."

REVIVE THE COURT JESTER

I hope the Government will not think just now about appointing a Poet Laureate. I hardly think they can be altogether in the right mood. The business just now before the country makes a very good detective story; but as a national epic it is a little depressing. Jingo literature always weakens a nation; but even healthy patriotic literature has its proper time and occasion. For instance, Mr. Newbolt (who has been suggested for the post) is a very fine poet; but I think his patriotic lyrics would just now rather jar upon a patriot. We are rather too much concerned about our practical seamanship to feel quite confident that Drake will return and "drum them up the Channel as he drummed them long ago." On the contrary, we have an uncomfortable feeling that Drake's ship might suddenly go to the bottom, because the capitalists have made Lloyd George abolish the Plimsoll Line. One could not, without being understood ironically, adjure the two party teams to-day to "play up, play up and play the game," or to "love the game more than the prize." And there is no national hero at this moment in the soldiering line—unless, perhaps, it is Major Archer-Shee— of whom anyone would be likely to say: "Sed miles; sed pro patria." There is, indeed, one beautiful poem of Mr. Newbolt's which may mingle faintly with one's thoughts in such times, but that, alas, is to a very different tune. I mean that one in which he echoes Turner's conception of the old wooden ship vanishing with all the valiant memories of the English:

There's a far bell ringing At the setting of the sun, And a phantom voice is singing Of the great days done. There's a far bell ringing, And a phantom voice is singing Of a fame forever clinging To the great days done. For the sunset breezes shiver, Temeraire, Temeraire, And she's fading down the river....

Well, well, neither you nor I know whether she is fading down the river or not. It is quite enough for us to know, as King Alfred did, that a great many pirates have landed on both banks of the Thames.

Praise and Prophecy Impossible
At this moment that is the only kind of patriotic poem that could satisfy the emotions of a patriotic person. But it certainly

is not the sort of poem that is expected from a Poet Laureate, either on the highest or the lowest theory of his office. He is either a great minstrel singing the victories of a great king, or he is a common Court official like the Groom of the Powder Closet. In the first case his praises should be true; in the second case they will nearly always be false; but in either case he must praise. And what there is for him to praise just now it would be precious hard to say. And if there is no great hope of a real poet, there is still less hope of a real prophet. What Newman called, I think, "The Prophetical Office," that is, the institution of an inspired protest even against an inspired religion, certainly would not do in modern England. The Court is not likely to keep a tame prophet in order to encourage him to be wild. It is not likely to pay a man to say that wolves shall howl in Downing-street and vultures build their nests in Buckingham Palace. So vast has been the progress of humanity that these two things are quite impossible. We cannot have a great poet praising kings. We cannot have a great prophet denouncing kings. So I have to fall back on a third suggestion.

The Field for a Fool

Instead of reviving the Court Poet, why not revive the Court Fool? He is the only person who could do any good at this moment either to the Royal or the judicial Courts. The present political situation is utterly unsuitable for the purposes of a great poet. But it is particularly suitable for the purposes of a great buffoon. The old jester was under certain privileges: you could not resent the jokes of a fool, just as you cannot resent the sermons of a curate. Now, what the present Government of England wants is neither serious praise nor serious denunciation; what it wants is satire. What it wants, in other words, is realism given with gusto. When King Louis the Eleventh unexpectedly visited his enemy, the Duke of Burgundy, with a small escort, the Duke's jester said he would give the King his fool's cap, for he was the fool now. And when the Duke replied with dignity, "And suppose I treat him with all proper respect?" the fool answered, "Then I will give it to you." That is the kind of thing that somebody ought to be free to say now. But if you say it now you will be fined a hundred pounds at the least.

Carson's Dilemma

For the things that have been happening lately are not merely things that one could joke about. They are themselves, truly and intrinsically, jokes. I mean that there is a sort of epigram of unreason in the situation itself, as there was in the situation where there was jam yesterday and jam to-morrow but never jam to-day. Take, for instance, the extraordinary case of Sir Edward Carson. The point is not whether we regard his attitude in Belfast as the defiance of a sincere and dogmatic rebel, or as the bluff of a party hack and mountebank. The point is not whether we regard his defence of the Government at the Old Bailey as a chivalrous and reluctant duty done as an advocate or a friend, or as a mere case of a lawyer selling his soul for a fat brief. The point is that whichever of the two actions we approve, and whichever of the four explanations we adopt, Sir Edward's position is still raving nonsense. On any argument, he cannot escape from his dilemma. It may be argued that laws and customs should be obeyed whatever our private feelings; and that it is an established custom to accept a brief in such a case. But then it is a somewhat more established custom to obey an Act of Parliament and to keep the peace. It may be argued that extreme misgovernment justifies men in Ulster or elsewhere in refusing to obey the law. But then it would justify them even more in refusing to appear professionally in a law court. Etiquette cannot be at once so unimportant that Carson may shoot at the King's uniform, and yet so important that he must always be ready to put on his own. The Government cannot be so disreputable that Carson need not lay down his gun, and yet so respectable that he is bound to put on his wig. Carson cannot at once be so fierce that he can kill in what he considers a good cause, and yet so meek that he must argue in what he considers a bad cause. Obedience or disobedience, conventional or unconventional, a solicitor's letter cannot be more sacred than the King's writ; a blue bag cannot be more rational than the British flag. The thing is rubbish read anyway, and the only difficulty is to get a joke good enough to express it. It is a case for the Court Jester. The phantasy of it could only be expressed by some huge ceremonial hoax. Carson ought to be crowned with the shamrocks and emeralds and followed by green-clad minstrels of the Clan-na-Gael, playing "The Wearing of the Green."

Belated Chattiness by Wireless

But all the recent events are like that. They are practical jokes. The jokes do not need to be made: they only need to be pointed out. You and I do not talk and act as the Isaacs brothers talked and acted, by their own most favourable account of themselves; and even their account of themselves was by no means favourable. You and I do not talk of meeting our own born brother "at a family function" as if he were some infinitely distant cousin whom we only met at Christmas. You and I, when we suddenly feel inclined for a chat with the same brother about his dinner and the Coal Strike, do not generally select either wireless telegraphy or the Atlantic Cable as the most obvious and economical channel for that outburst of belated chattiness. You and I do not talk, if it is proposed to start a railway between Catsville and Dogtown, as if the putting up of a station at Dogtown could have no kind of economic effect on the putting up of a station at Catsville. You and I do not think it candid to say that when we are at one end of a telephone we have no sort of connection with the other end. These things have got into the region of farce; and should be dealt with farcically, not even ferociously.

A Fool Who Shall Be Free

In the Roman Republic there was a Tribune of the People, whose person was inviolable like an ambassador's. There was much the same idea in Becket's attempt to remove the Priest, who was then the popular champion, from the ordinary courts. We shall have no Tribune; for we have no republic. We shall have no Priest; for we have no religion. The best we deserve or can expect is a Fool who shall be free; and who shall deliver us with laughter.

THE ART OF MISSING THE POINT

Missing the point is a very fine art; and has been carried to something like perfection by politicians and Pressmen to-day. For the point is generally a very sharp point; and is, moreover, sharp at both ends. That is to say that both parties would probably impale themselves in an uncomfortable manner if they did not manage to avoid it altogether. I have just been looking at the election address of the official Liberal candidate for the part of the country in which I live; and though it is, if anything, rather more logical and free from cant than most other documents of the sort it is an excellent example of missing the point. The candidate has to go boring on about Free Trade and Land Reform and Education; and nobody reading it could possibly imagine that in the town of Wycombe, where the poll will be declared, the capital of the Wycombe division of Bucks which the candidate is contesting, centre of the important and vital trade on which it has thriven, a savage struggle about justice has been raging for months past between the poor and rich, as real as the French Revolution. The man offering himself at Wycombe as representative of the Wycombe division simply says nothing about it at all. It is as if a man at the crisis of the French Terror had offered himself as a deputy for the town of Paris, and had said nothing about the Monarchy, nothing about the Republic, nothing about the massacres, nothing about the war; but had explained with great clearness his views on the suppression of the Jansenists, the literary style of Racine, the suitability of Turenae for the post of commander-in-chief, and the religious reflections of Madame de Maintenon. For, at their best, the candidate's topics are not topical. Home Rule is a very good thing, and modern education is a very bad thing; but neither of them are things that anybody is talking about in High Wycombe. This is the first and simplest way of missing the point: deliberately to avoid and ignore it.

The Candid Candidate

It would be an amusing experiment, by the way, to go to the point instead of avoiding it. What fun it would be to stand as a strict Party candidate, but issue a perfectly frank and cynical Election Address. Mr. Mosley's address begins, "Gentlemen,—

Sir Alfred Cripps having been chosen for a high judicial position and a seat in the House of Lords, a by-election now becomes necessary, and the electors of South Bucks are charged with the responsible duty of electing, etc., etc." But suppose there were another candidate whose election address opened in a plain, manly style, like this: "Gentlemen,—In the sincere hope of being myself chosen for a high judicial position or a seat in the House of Lords, or considerably increasing my private fortune by some Government appointment, or, at least, inside information about the financial prospects, I have decided that it is worth my while to disburse large sums of money to you on various pretexts, and, with even more reluctance to endure the bad speaking and bad ventilation of the Commons' House of Parliament, so help me God. I have very pronounced convictions on various political questions; but I will not trouble my fellow-citizens with them, since I have quite made up my mind to abandon any or all of them if requested to do so by the upper classes. The electors are therefore charged with the entirely irresponsible duty of electing a Member; or, in other words, I ask my neighbours round about this part, who know I am not a bad chap in many ways, to do me a good turn in my business, just as I might ask them to change a sovereign. My election will have no conceivable kind of effect on anything or anybody except myself; so I ask, as man to man, the Electors of the Southern or Wycombe Division of the County of Buckingham to accept a ride in one of my motor-cars; and poll early to please a pal—God Save the King." I do not know whether you or I would be elected if we presented ourselves with an election address of that kind; but we should have had our fun and (comparatively speaking) saved our souls; and I have a strong suspicion that we should be elected or rejected on a mechanical majority like anybody else; nobody having dreamed of reading an election address any more than an advertisement of a hair restorer.

Tyranny and Head-Dress

But there is another and more subtle way in which we may miss the point; and that is, not by keeping a dead silence about it, but by being just witty enough to state it wrong. Thus, some of the Liberal official papers have almost screwed up their courage to the sticking-point about the bestial coup d'etat in South Africa. They have screwed up their courage to the sticking-point; and it has stuck. It cannot get any further; because it has missed the main point. The modern Liberals make their feeble attempts to attack the introduction of slavery into South Africa by the Dutch and the Jews, by a very typical evasion of the vital fact. The vital fact is simply slavery. Most of these Dutchmen have always felt like slave-owners. Most of these Jews have always felt like slaves. Now that they are on top, they have a particular and curious kind of impudence, which is only known among slaves. But the Liberal journalists will do their best to suggest that the South African wrong consisted in what they call Martial Law. That is, that there is something specially wicked about men doing an act of cruelty in khaki or in vermilion, but not if it is done in dark blue with pewter buttons. The tyrant who wears a busby or a forage cap is abominable; the tyrant who wears a horsehair wig is excusable. To be judged by soldiers is hell; but to be judged by lawyers is paradise.

Now the point must not be missed in this way. What is wrong with the tyranny in Africa is not that it is run by soldiers. It would be quite as bad, or worse, if it were run by policemen. What is wrong is that, for the first time since Pagan times, private men are being forced to work for a private man. Men are being punished by imprisonment or exile for refusing to accept a job. The fact that Botha can ride on a horse, or fire off a gun, makes him better rather than worse than any man like Sidney Webb or Philip Snowden, who attempt the same slavery by much less manly methods. The Liberal Party will try to divert the whole discussion to one about what they call militarism. But the very terms of modern politics contradict it. For when we talk of real rebels against the present system we call them Militants. And there will be none in the Servile State.

THE SERVILE STATE AGAIN

I read the other day, in a quotation from a German newspaper, the highly characteristic remark that Germany having annexed Belgium would soon re-establish its commerce and prosperity, and that, in particular, arrangements were already being made for introducing into the new province the German laws for the protection of workmen.

I am quite content with that paragraph for the purpose of any controversy about what is called German atrocity. If men I know had not told me they had themselves seen the bayoneting of a baby; if the most respectable refugees did not bring with them stories of burning cottages—yes, and of burning cottagers as well; if doctors did not report what they do report of the condition of girls in the hospitals; if there were no facts; if there were no photographs, that one phrase I have quoted would be quite sufficient to satisfy me that the Prussians are tyrants; tyrants in a peculiar and almost insane sense which makes them pre-eminent among the evil princes of the earth. The first and most striking feature is a stupidity that rises into a sort of ghastly innocence. The protection of workmen! Some workmen, perhaps, might have a fancy for being protected from shrapnel; some might be glad to put up an umbrella that would ward off things dropping from the gentle Zeppelin in heaven upon the place beneath. Some of these discontented proletarians have taken the same view as Vandervelde their leader, and are now energetically engaged in protecting themselves along the line of the Yser; I am glad to say not altogether without success. It is probable that nearly all of the Belgian workers would, on the whole, prefer to be protected against bombs, sabres, burning cities, starvation, torture, and the treason of wicked kings. In short, it is probable—it is at least possible, impious as is the idea—that they would prefer to be protected against Germans and all they represent. But if a Belgian workman is told that he is not to be protected against Germans, but actually to be protected by Germans, I think he may be excused for staring. His first impulse, I imagine, will be to ask, "Against whom? Are there any worse people to come along?"

But apart from the hellish irony of this humanitarian idea, the question it raises is really one of solid importance for people whose politics are more or less like ours. There is a very urgent point in that question, "Against whom would the Belgian workmen be protected by the German laws?" And if we pursue it, we shall be enabled to analyse something of that poison— very largely a Prussian poison—which has long been working in our own commonwealth, to the enslavement of the weak and the secret strengthening of the strong. For the Prussian armies are, pre-eminently, the advance guard of the Servile State. I say this scientifically, and quite apart from passion or even from preference. I have no illusions about either Belgium or England. Both have been stained with the soot of Capitalism and blinded with the smoke of mere Colonial ambition; both have been caught at a disadvantage in such modern dirt and disorder; both have come out much better than I should have expected countries so modern and so industrial to do. But in England and Belgium there is Capitalism mixed up with a great many other things, strong things and things that pursue other aims; Clericalism, for instance, and militant Socialism in Belgium; Trades Unionism and sport and the remains of real aristocracy in England. But Prussia is Capitalism; that is, a gradually solidifying slavery; and that majestic unity with which she moves, dragging all the dumb Germanies after her, is due to the fact that her Servile State is complete, while ours is incomplete. There are not mutinies; there are not even mockeries; the voice of national self-criticism has been extinguished forever. For this people is already permanently cloven into a higher and a lower class: in its industry as much as its army. Its employers are, in the strictest and most sinister sense, captains of industry. Its proletariat is, in the truest and most pitiable sense, an army of labour. In that atmosphere masters bear upon them the signs that they are more than men; and to insult an officer is death.

If anyone ask how this extreme and unmistakable subordination of the employed to the employers is brought about, we all know the answer. It is brought about by hunger and hardness of heart, accelerated by a certain kind of legislation, of which we have had a good deal lately in England, but which was almost invariably borrowed from Prussia. Mr. Herbert Samuel's suggestion that the poor should be able to put their money in little boxes and not be able to get it out again is a sort of standing symbol of all the rest. I have forgotten how the poor were going to benefit eventually by what is for them indistinguishable from dropping sixpence down a drain. Perhaps they were going to get it back some day; perhaps when they could produce a hundred coupons out of the Daily Citizen; perhaps when they got their hair cut; perhaps when they consented to be inoculated, or trepanned, or circumcised, or something. Germany is full of this sort of legislation; and if you asked an innocent German, who honestly believed in it, what it was, he would answer that it was for the protection of workmen.

And if you asked again "Their protection from what?" you would have the whole plan and problem of the Servile State plain in front of you. Whatever notion there is, there is no notion whatever of protecting the employed person *from his employer*. Much less is there any idea of his ever being anywhere except under an employer. Whatever the Capitalist wants he gets. He may have the sense to want washed and well-fed labourers rather than dirty and feeble ones, and the restrictions may happen to exist in the form of laws from the Kaiser or by-laws from the Krupps. But the Kaiser will not offend the Krupps, and the Krupps will not offend the Kaiser. Laws of this kind, then, do not attempt to protect workmen against the injustice of the Capitalist as the English Trade Unions did. They do not attempt to protect workmen against the injustice of the State as the mediaeval guilds did. Obviously they cannot protect workmen against the foreign invader—especially when (as in the comic case of Belgium) they are imposed by the foreign invader. What then are such laws designed to protect workmen against? Tigers, rattlesnakes, hyenas?

Oh, my young friends; oh, my Christian brethren, they are designed to protect this poor person from something which to those of established rank is more horrid than many hyenas. They are designed, my friends, to protect a man from himself— from something that the masters of the earth fear more than famine or war, and which Prussia especially fears as everything fears that which would certainly be its end. They are meant to protect a man against himself—that is, they are meant to protect a man against his manhood.

And if anyone reminds me that there is a Socialist Party in Germany, I reply that there isn't.

THE EMPIRE OF THE IGNORANT

That anarchic future which the more timid Tories professed to fear has already fallen upon us. We are ruled by ignorant people. But the most ignorant people in modern Britain are to be found in the upper class, the middle class, and especially the upper middle class. I do not say it with the smallest petulance or even distaste; these classes are often really beneficent in their breeding or their hospitality, or their humanity to animals.

There is still no better company than the young at the two Universities, or the best of the old in the Army or some of the other services. Also, of course, there are exceptions in the matter of learning; real scholars like Professor Gilbert Murray or Professor Phillimore are not ignorant, though they *are* gentlemen. But when one looks up at any mass of the wealthier and more powerful classes, at the Grand Stand at Epsom, at the windows of Park-lane, at the people at a full-dress debate or a fashionable wedding, we shall be safe in saying that they are, for the most part, the most ill-taught, or untaught, creatures in these islands.

Literally Illiterate

It is indeed their feeble boast that they are not literally illiterate. They are always saying the ancient barons could not sign their own names—for they know less of history perhaps than of anything else. The modern barons, however, can sign their own names—or someone else's for a change. They can sign their own names; and that is about all they can do. They cannot face a fact, or follow an argument, or feel a tradition; but, least of all, can they, upon any persuasion, read through a plain impartial book, English or foreign, that is not specially written to soothe their panic or to please their pride. Looking up at these seats of the mighty I can only say, with something of despair, what Robert Lowe said of the enfranchised workmen: "We must educate our masters."

I do not mean this as paradoxical, or even as symbolical; it is simply tame and true. The modern English rich know nothing about things, not even about the things to which they appeal. Compared with them, the poor are pretty sure to get some enlightenment, even if they cannot get liberty; they must at least be technical. An old apprentice learnt a trade, even if his master came like any Turk and banged him most severely. The old housewife knew which side her bread was buttered, even if it were so thin as to be almost imperceptible. The old sailor knew the ropes; even if he knew the rope's end. Consequently, when any of these revolted, they were concerned with things they knew, pains, practical impossibilities, or the personal record.

But They Know

The apprentice cried "Clubs?" and cracked his neighbours' heads with the precision and fineness of touch which only manual craftsmanship can give. The housewives who flatly refused to cook the hot dinner knew how much or how little, cold meat there was in the house. The sailor who defied discipline by mutinying at the Nore did not defy discipline in the sense of falling off the rigging or letting the water into the hold. Similarly the modern proletariat, however little it may know, knows what it is talking about.

But the curious thing about the educated class is that exactly what it does not know is what it is talking about. I mean that it is startlingly ignorant of those special things which it is supposed to invoke and keep inviolate. The things that workmen invoke may be uglier, more acrid, more sordid; but they know all about them. They know enough arithmetic to know that prices have risen; the kind Levantine gentleman is always there to make them fully understand the meaning of an interest sum; and the landlord will define Rent as rigidly as Ricardo. The doctors can always tell them the Latin for an empty stomach; and when the poor man is treated for the time with some human respect (by the Coronet) it almost seems a pity he is not alive to hear how legally he died.

Against this bitter shrewdness and bleak realism in the suffering classes it is commonly supposed that the more leisured classes stand for certain legitimate ideas which also have their place in life; such as history, reverence, the love of the land. Well, it might be no bad thing to have something, even if it were something narrow, that testified to the truths of religion or patriotism. But such narrow things in the past have always at least known their own history; the bigot knew his catechism; the patriot knew his way home. The astonishing thing about the modern rich is their real and sincere ignorance—especially of the things they like.

No!

Take the most topical case you can find in any drawing-room: Belfast. Ulster is most assuredly a matter of history; and there is a sense in which Orange resistance is a matter of religion. But go and ask any of the five hundred fluttering ladies at a garden party (who find Carson so splendid and Belfast so thrilling) what it is all about, when it began, where it came from, what it really maintains? What was the history of Ulster? What is the religion of Belfast? Do any of them know where Ulstermen were in Grattan's time; do any of them know what was the "Protestantism" that came from Scotland to that isle; could any of them tell what part of the old Catholic system it really denied?

It was generally something that the fluttering ladies find in their own Anglican churches every Sunday. It were vain to ask them to state the doctrines of the Calvinist creed; they could not state the doctrines of their own creed. It were vain to tell them to read the history of Ireland; they have never read the history of England. It would matter as little that they do not know these things, as that I do not know German; but then German is not the only thing I am supposed to know. History and ritual are the only things aristocrats are supposed to know; and they don't know them.

Smile and Smile

I am not fed on turtle soup and Tokay because of my exquisite intimacy with the style and idiom of Heine and Richter. The English governing class is fed on turtle soup and Tokay to represent the past, of which it is literally ignorant, as I am of German irregular verbs; and to represent the religious traditions of the State, when it does not know three words of theology, as I do not know three words of German.

This is the last insult offered by the proud to the humble. They rule them by the smiling terror of an ancient secret. They smile and smile; but they have forgotten the secret.

THE SYMBOLISM OF KRUPP

The curious position of the Krupp firm in the awful story developing around us is not quite sufficiently grasped. There is a kind of academic clarity of definition which does not see the proportions of things for which everything falls within a definition, and nothing ever breaks beyond it. To this type of mind (which is valuable when set to its special and narrow work) there is no such thing as an exception that proves the rule. If I vote for confiscating some usurer's millions I am doing, they say, precisely what I should be doing if I took pennies out of a blind man's hat. They are both denials of the principle of private property, and are equally right and equally wrong, according to our view of that principle. I should find a great many distinctions to draw in such a matter. First, I should say that taking a usurer's money by proper authority is not robbery, but recovery of stolen goods. Second, I should say that even if there were no such thing as personal property, there would still be such a thing as personal dignity, and different modes of robbery would diminish it in very different ways. Similarly, there is a truth, but only a half-truth, in the saying that all modern Powers alike rely on the Capitalist and make war on the lines of Capitalism. It is true, and it is disgraceful. But it is *not* equally true and equally disgraceful. It is not true that Montenegro is as much ruled by financiers as Prussia, just as it is not true that as many men in the Kaiserstrasse, in Berlin, wear long knives in their belts as wear them in the neighbourhood of the Black Mountain. It is not true that every peasant from one of the old Russian communes is the immediate servant of a rich man, as is every employee of Mr. Rockefeller. It is as false as the statement that no poor people in America can read or write. There is an element of Capitalism in all modern countries, as there is an element of illiteracy in all modern countries. There are some who think that the number of our fellow-citizens who can sign their names ought to comfort us for the extreme fewness of those who have anything in the bank to sign it for, but I am not one of these.

In any case, the position of Krupp has certain interesting aspects. When we talk of Army contractors as among the base but active actualities of war, we commonly mean that while the contractor benefits by the war, the war, on the whole, rather suffers by the contractor. We regard this unsoldierly middleman with disgust, or great anger, or contemptuous acquiescence, or commercial dread and silence, according to our personal position and character. But we nowhere think of him as having anything to do with fighting in the final sense. Those worthy and wealthy persons who employ women's labour at a few shillings a week do not do it to obtain the best clothes for the soldiers, but to make a sufficient profit on the worst. The only argument is whether such clothes are just good enough for the soldiers, or are too bad for anybody or anything. We tolerate the contractor, or we do not tolerate him; but no one admires him especially, and certainly no one gives him any credit for any success in the war. Confessedly or unconfessedly we knock his profits, not only off what goes to the taxpayer, but what goes to the soldier. We know the Army will not fight any better, at least, because the clothes they wear were stitched by wretched women who could hardly see; or because their boots were made by harassed helots, who never had time to think. In war-time it is very widely confessed that Capitalism is not a good way of ruling a patriotic or self-respecting people, and all sorts of other things, from strict State organisation to quite casual personal charity, are hastily substituted for it. It is recognised that the "great employer," nine times out of ten, is no more than the schoolboy or the page who pilfers tarts and sweets from the dishes as they go up and down. How angry one is with him depends on temperament, on the stage of the dinner—also on the number of tarts.

Now here comes in the real and sinister significance of Krupps. There are many capitalists in Europe as rich, as vulgar, as selfish, as rootedly opposed to any fellowship of the fortunate and unfortunate. But there is no other capitalist who claims, or can pretend to claim, that he has very appreciably *helped* the activities of his people in war. I will suppose that Lipton did not deserve the very severe criticisms made on his firm by Mr. Justice Darling; but, however blameless he was, nobody can suppose that British soldiers would charge better with the bayonet because they had some particular kind of groceries inside them. But Krupp can make a plausible claim that the huge infernal machines to which his country owes nearly all of its successes could only have been produced under the equally infernal conditions of the modern factory and the urban and proletarian civilisation. That is why the victory of Germany would be simply the victory of Krupp, and the victory of Krupp would be simply the victory of Capitalism. There, and there alone, Capitalism would be able to point to something done successfully for a whole nation—done (as it would certainly maintain) better than small free States or natural democracies could have done it. I confess I think the modern Germans morally second-rate, and I think that even war, when it is conducted most successfully by machinery, is second-rate war. But this second-rate war will become not only the first but the only brand, if the cannon of Krupp should conquer; and, what is very much worse, it will be the only intelligent answer that any capitalist has yet given against our case that Capitalism is as wasteful and as weak as it is certainly wicked. I do not fear any such finality, for I happen to believe in the kind of men who fight best with bayonets and whose fathers hammered their own pikes for the French Revolution.

THE TOWER OF BEBEL

Among the cloudy and symbolic stories in the beginning of the Bible there is one about a tower built with such vertical energy as to take a hold on heaven, but ruined and resulting only in a confusion of tongues. The story might be interpreted in many ways—religiously, as meaning that spiritual insolence starts all human separations; irreligiously, as meaning that the inhuman heavens grudge man his magnificent dream; or merely satirically as suggesting that all attempts to reach a higher agreement always end in more disagreement than there was before. It might be taken by the partially intelligent Kensitite as a judgment on Latin Christians for talking Latin. It might be taken by the somewhat less intelligent Professor Harnack as a final proof that all prehistoric humanity talked German. But when all was said, the symbol would remain that a plain tower, as straight as a sword, as simple as a lily, did nevertheless produce the deepest divisions that have been known among men. In any case we of the world in revolt—Syndicalists, Socialists, Guild Socialists, or whatever we call ourselves— have no need to worry about the scripture or the allegory. We have the reality. For whatever reason, what is said to have happened to the people of Shinak has precisely and practically happened to us.

None of us who have known Socialists (or rather, to speak more truthfully, none of us who have been Socialists) can entertain the faintest doubt that a fine intellectual sincerity lay behind what was called "L'Internationale." It was really felt that Socialism was universal like arithmetic. It was too true for idiom or turn of phrase. In the formula of Karl Marx men could find that frigid fellowship which they find when they agree that two and two make four. It was almost as broadminded as a religious dogma.

Yet this universal language has not succeeded, at a moment of crisis, in imposing itself on the whole world. Nay, it has not, at the moment of crisis, succeeded in imposing itself on its own principal champions. Herve is not talking Economic Esperanto; he is talking French. Bebel is not talking Economic Esperanto; he is talking German. Blatchford is not talking Economic Esperanto; he is talking English, and jolly good English, too. I do not know whether French or Flemish was Vandervelde's nursery speech, but I am quite certain he will know more of it after this struggle than he knew before. In short, whether or no there be a new union of hearts, there has really and truly been a new division of tongues.

How are we to explain this singular truth, even if we deplore it? I dismiss with fitting disdain the notion that it is a mere result of military terrorism or snobbish social pressure. The Socialist leaders of modern Europe are among the most sincere men in history; and their Nationalist note in this affair has had the ring of their sincerity. I will not waste time on the speculation that Vandervelde is bullied by Belgian priests; or that Blatchford is frightened of the horse-guards outside Whitehall. These great men support the enthusiasm of their conventional countrymen because they share it; and they share it because there is (though perhaps only at certain great moments) such a thing as pure democracy.

Timour the Tartar, I think, celebrated some victory with a tower built entirely out of human skulls; perhaps he thought *that* would reach to heaven. But there is no cement in such building; the veins and ligaments that hold humanity together have long fallen away; the skulls will roll impotently at a touch; and ten thousand more such trophies could only make the tower taller and crazier. I think the modern official apparatus of "votes" is very like that tottering monument. I think the Tartar "counted heads," like an electioneering agent. Sometimes when I have seen from the platform of some paltry party meeting the rows and rows of grinning upturned faces, I have felt inclined to say, as the poet does in the "The Vision of Sin"—"Welcome fellow-citizens, Hollow hearts and empty heads."

Not that the people were personally hollow or empty, but they had come on a hollow and empty business: to help the good Mr. Binks to strengthen the Insurance Act against the wicked Mr. Jinks who would only promise to fortify the Insurance Act. That night it did not blow the democratic gale. Yet it can blow on these as on others; and when it does blow men learn many things. I, for one, am not above learning them.

The Marxian dogma which simplifies all conflicts to the Class War is so much nobler a thing than the nose-counting of the parliaments that one must apologise for the comparison. And yet there is a comparison. When we used to say that there were so many thousands of Socialists in Germany, we were counting by skulls. When we said that the majority consisting of Proletarians would be everywhere opposed to the minority, consisting of Capitalists, we were counting by skulls. Why, yes; if all men's heads had been cut off from the rest of them, as they were by the good sense and foresight of Timour the Tartar; if they had no hearts or bellies to be moved; no hand that flies up to ward off a weapon, no foot that can feel a familiar soil—if things were so the Marxian calculation would be not only complete but correct. As we know to-day, the Marxian calculation is complete, but it is not correct.

Now, this is the answer to the questions of some kind critics, whose actual words I have not within reach at the moment, about whether my democracy meant the rule of the majority over the minority. It means the rule of the rule—the rule of the rule over the exception. When a nation finds a soul it clothes it with a body, and does verily act like one living thing. There is nothing to be said about those who are out of it, except that they are out of it. After talking about it in the abstract for decades, this is Democracy, and it is marvellous in our eyes. It is not the difference between ninety-nine persons and a hundred persons; it is one person—the people. I do not know or care how many or how few of the Belgians like or dislike the pictures of Wiertz. They could not be either justified or condemned by a mere majority of Belgians. But I am very certain that the defiance to Prussia did not come from a majority of Belgians. It came from Belgium one and indivisible—atheists, priests, princes of the blood, Frenchified shopkeepers, Flemish boors, men, women, and children, and the sooner we understand that this sort of thing can happen the better for us. For it is this spontaneous spiritual fellowship of communities under certain conditions to which the four or five most independent minds of Europe willingly bear witness to-day.

But is there no exception: is there no one faithful among the unfaithful found? Is no great Socialist politician still untouched by the patriotism of the vulgar? Why, yes; the rugged Ramsay MacDonald, scarred with a hundred savage fights against the capitalist parties, still lifts up his horny hand for peace. What further need have we of witnesses? I, for my part, am quite satisfied, and do not doubt that Mr. MacDonald will be as industrious in damping down democracy in this form as in every other.

A REAL DANGER

Heaven forbid that I should once more wade in those swamps of logomachy and tautology in which the old guard of the Determinists still seem to be floundering. The question of Fate and Free Will can never attain to a conclusion, though it may attain to a conviction. The shortest philosophic summary is that both cause and choice are ultimate ideas within us, and that if one man denies choice because it seems contrary to cause, the other man has quite as much right to deny cause because it seems contrary to choice. The shortest ethical summary is that Determinism either affects conduct or it does not. If it does not, it is morally not worth preaching; if it does, it must affect conduct in the direction of impotence and submission. A writer in the "Clarion" says that the reformer cannot help trying to reform, nor the Conservative help his Conservatism. But suppose the reformer tries to reform the Conservative and turn him into another reformer? Either he can, in which case Determinism has made no difference at all, or he can't, in which case it can only have made reformers more hopeless and Conservatives more obstinate. And the shortest practical and political summary is that working men, most probably, will soon be much too busy using their Free Will to stop to prove that they have got it. Nevertheless, I like to watch the Determinist in the "Clarion" Cockpit every week, as busy as a squirrel—in a cage. But being myself a squirrel (leaping lightly from bough to bough) and preferring the form of activity which occasionally ends in nuts, I should not intervene in the matter even indirectly, except upon a practical point. And the point I have in mind is practical to the extent of deadly peril. It is another of the numerous new ways in which the restless rich, now walking the world with an awful insomnia, may manage to catch us napping.

Must Be a Mystery

There are two letters in the "Clarion" this week which in various ways interest me very much. One is concerned to defend Darwin against the scientific revolt against him that was led by Samuel Butler, and among other things it calls Bernard Shaw a back number. Well, most certainly "The Origin of

Species" is a back number, in so far as any honest and interesting book ever can be; but in pure philosophy nothing can be out of date, since the universe must be a mystery even to the believer. There is, however, one condition of things in which I do call it relevant to describe somebody as behind the times. That is when the man in question, thinking of some state of affairs that has passed away, is really helping the very things he would like to hinder. The principles cannot alter, but the problems can. Thus, I should call a man behind the times who, in the year 1872, pleaded for the peaceful German peasants against the triumphant militarism of Napoleon. Or I should call a man out of date who, in the year 1892, wished for a stronger Navy to compete with the Navy of Holland, because it had once swept the sea and sailed up the Thames. And I certainly call a man or a movement out of date that, in the year 1914, when we few are fighting a giant machine, strengthened with all material wealth and worked with all the material sciences, thinks that our chief danger is from an excess of moral and religious responsibility. He reminds me of Mr. Snodgrass, who had the presence of mind to call out "Fire!" when Mr. Pickwick fell through the ice.

The other letter consists of the usual wiredrawn argument for fatalism. Man cannot imagine the universe being created, and therefore is "compelled by his reason" to think the universe without beginning or end, which (I may remark) he cannot imagine either. But the letter ends with something much more ominous than bad metaphysics. Here, in the middle of the "Clarion," in the centre of a clean and combative democratic sheet, I meet again my deplorable old acquaintance, the scientific criminologist. "The so-called evil-doer should not be punished for his acts, but restrained." In forty-eight hours I could probably get a petition to that effect signed by millionaires. A short time ago a Bill was introduced to hold irresponsible and "restrain" a whole new class of people, who were "incapable of managing their affairs with prudence." Read the supporters' names on the back of that Bill, and see what sort of democrats they were.

Now, clearing our heads of what is called popular science (which means going to sleep to a lullaby of long words), let us use our own brains a little, and ask ourselves what is the real difference between punishing a man and restraining him. The material difference may be any or none; for punishment may be very mild, and restraint may be very ruthless. The man, of course, must dislike one as much as the other, or it would not be necessary to restrain him at all. And I assure you he will get no great glow of comfort out of your calling him irresponsible after you have made him impotent. A man does not necessarily feel more free and easy in a straight waistcoat than in a stone cell. The moral difference is that a man can be punished for a crime because he is born a citizen; while he can be constrained because he is born a slave. But one arresting and tremendous difference towers over all these doubtful or arguable differences. There is one respect, vital to all our liberties and all our lives, in which the new restraint would be different from the old punishment. It is of this that the plutocrats will take advantage.

The Plain Difference

The perfectly plain difference is this. All punishment, even the most horrible, proceeds upon the assumption that the extent of the evil is known, and that a certain amount of expiation goes with it. Even if you hang the man, you cannot hang him twice. Even if you burn him, you cannot burn him for a month. And in the case of all ordinary imprisonments, the whole aim of free institutions from the beginning of the world has been to insist that a man shall be convicted of a definite crime and confined for a definite period. But the moment you admit this notion of medical restraint, you must in fairness admit that it may go on as long as the authorities choose to think (or say) that it ought to go on. The man's punishment refers to the past, which is supposed to have been investigated, and which, in some degree at least, has been investigated. But his restraint refers to the future, which his doctors, keepers, and wardens have yet to investigate. The simple result will be that, in the scientific Utopia of the "Clarion," men like Mann or Syme or Larkin will not be put in prison because of what they have done. They will be kept in prison because of what they might do. Indeed, the builders of the new tyranny have already come very near to avowing this scientific and futurist method. When the lawyers tried to stop the "Suffragette" from appearing at all, they practically said: "We do not know your next week's crime, because it isn't committed yet; but we are scientifically certain you have the criminal type. And by the sublime and unalterable laws of heredity, all your poor little papers will inherit it."

This is a purely practical question; and that is why I insist on it, even in such strenuous times. The writers on the "Clarion" have a perfect right to think Christianity is the foe of freedom, or even that the stupidity and tyranny of the present Government is due to the monkish mysticism of Lord Morley and Mr. John M. Robertson. They have a right to think the theory of Determinism as true as Calvin thought it. But I do not like seeing them walk straight into the enormous iron trap set open by the Capitalists, who find it convenient to make our law even more lawless than it is. The rich men want a scientist to write them a *lettre de cachet* as a doctor writes a prescription. And so they wish to seal up in a public gaol the scandals of a private asylum. Yes; the writers on the "Clarion" are indeed claiming irresponsibility for human beings. But it is the governments that will be irresponsible, not the governed.

But I will tell them one small secret in conclusion. There is nothing whatever wrong in the ancient and universal idea of Punishment—except that we are not punishing the right people.

THE DREGS OF PURITANISM

One peculiarity of the genuine kind of enemy of the people is that his slightest phrase is clamorous with all his sins. Pride, vain-glory, and hypocrisy seem present in his very grammar; in his very verbs or adverbs or prepositions, as well as in what he says, which is generally bad enough. Thus I see that a Nonconformist pastor in Bromley has been talking about the pathetic little presents of tobacco sent to the common soldiers. This is how he talks about it. He is reported as having said, "By the help of God, they wanted this cigarette business stopped." How one could write a volume on that sentence, a great thick volume called "The Decline of the English Middle Class." In taste, in style, in philosophy, in feeling, in political project, the horrors of it are as unfathomable as hell.

First, to begin with the trifle, note something slipshod and vague in the mere verbiage, typical of those who prefer a catchword to a creed. "This cigarette business" might mean anything. It might mean Messrs. Salmon and Gluckstein's business. But the pastor at Bromley will not interfere with that, for the indignation of his school of thought, even when it is sincere, always instinctively and unconsciously swerves aside from anything that is rich and powerful like the partners in a big business, and strikes instead something that is poor and nameless like the soldiers in a trench. Nor does the expression make clear who "they" are—whether the inhabitants of Britain or the inhabitants of Bromley, or the inhabitants of this one crazy tabernacle in Bromley; nor is it evident how it is going to be stopped or who is being asked to stop it. All these things are trifles compared to the more terrible offences of the phrase; but they are not without their social and historical interest. About the beginning of the nineteenth century the wealthy Puritan class, generally the class of the employers of labour, took a line of argument which was narrow, but not nonsensical. They saw the relation of rich and poor quite coldly as a contract, but they saw that a contract holds both ways. The Puritans of the middle class, in short, did in some sense start talking and thinking for themselves. They are still talking. They have long ago left off thinking. They talk about the loyalty of workmen to their employers, and God knows what rubbish; and the first small certainty about the reverend gentleman whose sentence I have quoted is that his brain stopped working as a clock stops, years and years ago.

Second, consider the quality of the religious literature! These people are always telling us that the English translated Bible is sufficient training for anyone in noble and appropriate diction; and so it is. Why, then, are they not trained? They are always telling us that Bunyan, the rude Midland tinker, is as much worth reading as Chaucer or Spenser; and so he is. Why, then, have they not read him? I cannot believe that anyone who had seen, even in a nightmare of the nursery, Apollyon straddling over the whole breadth of the way could really write like that about a cigarette. By the help of God, they wanted this cigarette business stopped. Therefore, with angels and archangels and the whole company of Heaven, with St. Michael, smiter of Satan and Captain of the Chivalry of God, with all the ardour of the seraphs and the flaming patience of the saints, we will have this cigarette business stopped. Where has all the tradition of the great religious literatures gone to that a man should come on such a bathos with such a bump?

Thirdly, of course, there is the lack of imaginative proportion, which rises into a sort of towering blasphemy. An enormous number of live young men are being hurt by shells, hurt by bullets, hurt by fever and hunger and horror of hope deferred; hurt by lance blades and sword blades and bayonet blades breaking into the bloody house of life. But Mr. Price (I think that's his name) is still anxious that they should not be hurt by cigarettes. That is the sort of maniacal isolation that can be found in the deserts of Bromley. That cigarettes are bad for the health is a very tenable opinion to which the minister is quite entitled. If he happens to think that the youth of Bromley smoke too many cigarettes, and that he has any influence in urging on them the unhealthiness of the habit, I should not blame him if he gave sermons or lectures about it (with magic-lantern slides), so long as it was in Bromley and about Bromley. Cigarettes may be bad for the health: bombs and bayonets and even barbed wire are not good for the health. I never met a doctor who recommended any of them. But the trouble with this sort of man is that he cannot adjust himself to the scale of things. He would do very good service if he would go among the rich aristocratic ladies and tell them not to take drugs in a chronic sense, as people take opium in China. But he would be doing very bad service if he were to go among the doctors and nurses on the field and tell them not to give drugs, as they give morphia in a hospital. But it is the whole hypothesis of war, it is its very nature and first principle, that the man in the trench is almost as much a suffering and abnormal person as the man in the hospital. Hit or unhit, conqueror or conquered, he is, by nature of the case, having less pleasure than is proper and natural to a man.

Fourth (for I need not dwell here on the mere diabolical idiocy that can regard beer or tobacco as in some way evil and unseemly in themselves), there is the most important element in this strange outbreak; at least, the most dangerous and the most important for us. There is that main feature in the degradation of the old middle class: the utter disappearance of its old appetite for liberty. Here there is no question of whether the men are to smoke cigarettes, or the women choose to send cigarettes, or even that the officers or doctors choose to allow cigarettes. The thing is to cease, and we may note one of the most recurrent ideas of the servile State: it is mentioned in the passive mood. It must be stopped, and we must not even ask who has stopped it!

THE TYRANNY OF BAD JOURNALISM

The amazing decision of the Government to employ methods quite alien to England, and rather belonging to the police of the Continent, probably arises from the appearance of papers which are lucid and fighting, like the papers of the Continent. The business may be put in many ways. But one way of putting it is simply to say that a monopoly of bad journalism is resisting the possibility of good journalism. Journalism is not the same thing as literature; but there is good and bad journalism, as there is good and bad literature, as there is good and bad football. For the last twenty years or so the plutocrats who govern England have allowed the English nothing but bad journalism. Very bad journalism, simply considered as journalism.

It always takes a considerable time to see the simple and central fact about anything. All sorts of things have been said about the modern Press, especially the Yellow Press; that it is Jingo or Philistine or sensational or wrongly inquisitive or vulgar or indecent or trivial; but none of these have anything really to do with the point.

The point about the Press is that it is not what it is called. It is not the "popular Press." It is not the public Press. It is not an organ of public opinion. It is a conspiracy of a very few millionaires, all sufficiently similar in type to agree on the limits of what this great nation (to which we belong) may know about itself and its friends and enemies. The ring is not quite complete; there are old-fashioned and honest papers: but it is sufficiently near to completion to produce on the ordinary purchaser of news the practical effects of a corner and a monopoly. He receives all his political information and all his political marching orders from what is by this time a sort of half-conscious secret society, with very few members, but a great deal of money.

This enormous and essential fact is concealed for us by a number of legends that have passed into common speech. There is the notion that the Press is flashy or trivial *because* it is popular. In other words, an attempt is made to discredit democracy by representing journalism as the natural literature of democracy. All this is cold rubbish. The democracy has no more to do with the papers than it has with the peerages. The millionaire newspapers are vulgar and silly because the millionaires are vulgar and silly. It is the proprietor, not the editor, not the sub-editor, least of all the reader, who is pleased with this monotonous prairie of printed words. The same slander on democracy can be noticed in the case of advertisements. There is many a tender old Tory imagination that vaguely feels that our streets would be hung with escutcheons and tapestries, if only the profane vulgar had not hung them with advertisements of Sapolio and Sunlight Soap. But advertisement does not come from the unlettered many. It comes from the refined few. Did you ever hear of a mob rising to placard the Town Hall with proclamations in favour of Sapolio? Did you ever see a poor, ragged man laboriously drawing and painting a picture on the wall in favour of Sunlight Soap—simply as a labour of love? It is nonsense; those who hang our public walls with ugly pictures are the same select few who hang their private walls with exquisite and expensive pictures. The vulgarisation of modern life has come from the governing class; from the highly educated class. Most of the people who have posters in Camberwell have peerages at Westminster. But the strongest instance of all is that which has been unbroken until lately, and still largely prevails; the ghastly monotony of the Press.

Then comes that other legend; the notion that men like the masters of the Newspaper Trusts "give the people what they want." Why, it is the whole aim and definition of a Trust that it gives the people what it chooses. In the old days, when Parliaments were free in England, it was discovered that one courtier was allowed to sell all the silk, and another to sell all the sweet wine. A member of the House of Commons humorously asked who was allowed to sell all the bread. I really tremble to think what that sarcastic legislator would have said if he had been put off with the modern nonsense about "gauging the public taste." Suppose the first courtier had said that, by his shrewd, self-made sense, he had detected that people had a vague desire for silk; and even a deep, dim human desire to pay so much a yard for it! Suppose the second courtier said that he had, by his own rugged intellect, discovered a general desire for wine: and that people bought his wine at his price—when they could buy no other! Suppose a third courtier had jumped up and said that people always bought his bread when they could get none anywhere else.

Well, that is a perfect parallel. "After bread, the need of the people is knowledge," said Danton. Knowledge is now a monopoly, and comes through to the citizens in thin and selected streams, exactly as bread might come through to a besieged city. Men must wish to know what is happening, whoever has the privilege of telling them. They must listen to the messenger, even if he is a liar. They must listen to the liar, even if he is a bore. The official journalist for some time past has been both a bore and a liar; but it was impossible until lately to neglect his sheets of news altogether. Lately the capitalist Press really has begun to be neglected; because its bad journalism was overpowering and appalling. Lately we have really begun to find out that capitalism cannot write, just as it cannot fight, or pray, or marry, or make a joke, or do any other stricken human thing. But this discovery has been quite recent. The capitalist newspaper was never actually unread until it was actually unreadable.

If you retain the servile superstition that the Press, as run by the capitalists, is popular (in any sense except that in which dirty water in a desert is popular), consider the case of the solemn articles in praise of the men who own newspapers—men of the type of Cadbury or Harmsworth, men of the type of the small club of millionaires. Did you ever hear a plain man in a tramcar or train talking about Carnegie's bright genial smile or Rothschild's simple, easy hospitality? Did you ever hear an ordinary citizen ask what was the opinion of Sir Joseph Lyons about the hopes and fears of this, our native land? These few small-minded men publish, papers to praise themselves. You could no more get an intelligent poor man to praise a millionaire's soul, except for hire, than you could get him to sell a millionaire's soap, except for hire. And I repeat that, though there are other aspects of the matter of the new plutocratic raid, one of the most important is mere journalistic jealousy. The Yellow Press is bad journalism: and wishes to stop the appearance of good journalism.

There is no average member of the public who would not prefer to have Lloyd George discussed as what he is, a Welshman of genius and ideals, strangely fascinated by bad fashion and bad finance, rather than discussed as what neither he nor anyone else ever was, a perfect democrat or an utterly detestable demagogue. There is no reader of a daily paper who would not feel more concern—and more respect—for Sir Rufus Isaacs as a man who has been a stockbroker, than as a man who happens to be Attorney-General. There is no man in the street who is not more interested in Lloyd George's investments than in his Land Campaign. There is no man in the street who could not understand (and like) Rufus Isaacs as a Jew better than he can possibly like him as a British statesman. There is no sane journalist alive who would say that the official account of Marconis would be better "copy" than the true account that such papers as this have dragged out. We have committed one crime against the newspaper proprietor which he will never forgive. We point out that his papers are dull. And we propose to print some papers that are interesting.

THE POETRY OF THE REVOLUTION

Everyone but a consistent and contented capitalist, who must be something pretty near to a Satanist, must rejoice at the spirit and success of the Battle of the Buses. But one thing about it which happens to please me particularly was that it was fought, in one aspect at least, on a point such as the plutocratic fool calls unpractical. It was fought about a symbol, a badge, a thing attended with no kind of practical results, like the flags for which men allow themselves to fall down dead, or the shrines for which men will walk some hundreds of miles from their homes. When a man has an eye for business, all that goes on on this earth in that style is simply invisible to him. But let us be charitable to the eye for business; the eye has been pretty well blacked this time.

But I wish to insist here that it is exactly what is called the unpractical part of the thing that is really the practical. The chief difference between men and the animals is that all men are artists; though the overwhelming majority of us are bad artists. As the old fable truly says, lions do not make statues; even the cunning of the fox can go no further than the accomplishment of leaving an exact model of the vulpine paw: and even that is an accomplishment which he wishes he hadn't got. There are Chryselephantine statues, but no purely elephantine ones. And, though we speak in a general way of an elephant trumpeting, it is only by human blandishments that he can be induced to play the drum. But man, savage or civilised, simple or complex always desires to see his own soul outside himself; in some material embodiment. He always wishes to point to a table in a temple, or a cloth on a stick, or a word on a scroll, or a badge on a coat, and say: "This is the best part of me. If need be, it shall be the rest of me that shall perish." This is the method which seems so unbusinesslike to the men with an eye to business. This is also the method by which battles are won.

The Symbolism of the Badge

The badge on a Trade Unionist's coat is a piece of poetry in the genuine, lucid, and logical sense in which Milton defined poetry (and he ought to know) when he said that it was simple, sensuous, and passionate. It is simple, because many understand the word "badge," who might not even understand the word "recognition." It is sensuous, because it is visible and tangible; it is incarnate, as all the good Gods have been; and it is passionate in this perfectly practical sense, which the man with an eye to business may some day learn more thoroughly than he likes, that there are men who will allow you to cross a word out in a theoretical document, but who will not allow you to pull a big button off their bodily clothing, merely because you have more money than they have. Now I think it is this sensuousness, this passion, and, above all, this simplicity that are most wanted in this promising revolt of our time. For this simplicity is perhaps the only thing in which the best type of recent revolutionists have failed. It has been our sorrow lately to salute the sunset of one of the very few clean and incorruptible careers in the most corruptible phase of Christendom. The death of Quelch naturally turns one's thoughts to those extreme Marxian theorists, who, whatever we may hold about their philosophy, have certainly held their honour like iron. And yet, even in this instant of instinctive reverence, I cannot feel that they were poetical enough, that is childish enough, to make a revolution. They had all the audacity needed for speaking to the despot; but not the simplicity needed for speaking to the democracy. They were always accused of being too bitter against the capitalist. But it always seemed to me that they were (quite unconsciously, of course) much too kind to him. They had a fatal habit of using long words, even on occasions when he might with propriety have been described in very short words. They called him a Capitalist when almost anybody in Christendom would have called him a cad. And "cad" is a word from the poetic vocabulary indicating rather a general and powerful reaction of the emotions than a status that could be defined in a work of economics. The capitalist, asleep in the sun, let such long words crawl all over him, like so many long, soft, furry caterpillars. Caterpillars cannot sting like wasps. And, in repeating that the old Marxians have been, perhaps, the best and bravest men of our time, I say also that they would have been better and braver still if they had never used a scientific word, and never read anything but fairy tales.

The Beastly Individualist

Suppose I go on to a ship, and the ship sinks almost immediately; but I (like the people in the Bab Ballads), by reason of my clinging to a mast, upon a desert island am eventually cast. Or rather, suppose I am not cast on it, but am kept bobbing about in the water, because the only man on the island is what some call an Individualist, and will not throw me a rope; though coils of rope of the most annoying elaboration and neatness are conspicuous beside him as he stands upon the shore. Now, it seems to me, that if, in my efforts to shout at this fellow-creature across the crashing breakers, I call his position the "insularistic position," and my position "the semi-amphibian position," much valuable time may be lost. I am not an amphibian. I am a drowning man. He is not an insularist, or an individualist. He is a beast. Or rather, he is worse than any beast can be. And if, instead of letting me drown, he makes me promise, while I am drowning, that if I come on shore it shall be as his bodily slave, having no human claims henceforward forever, then, by the whole theory and practice of capitalism, he becomes a capitalist, he also becomes a cad.

Now, the language of poetry is simpler than that of prose; as anyone can see who has read what the old-fashioned protestant used to call confidently "his" Bible. And, being simpler, it is also truer; and, being truer, it is also fiercer. And, for most of the infamies of our time, there is really nothing plain enough, except the plain language of poetry. Take, let us say, the ease of the recent railway disaster, and the acquittal of the capitalists' interest. It is not a scientific problem for us to investigate. It is a crime committed before our eyes; committed, perhaps, by blind men or maniacs, or men hypnotised, or men in some other ways unconscious; but committed in broad daylight, so that the corpse is bleeding on our door-step. Good lives were lost, because good lives do not pay; and bad coals do pay. It seems simply impossible to get any other meaning out of the matter except that. And, if in human history there be anything simple and anything horrible, it seems to have been present in this matter. If, even after some study and understanding of the old religious passions which were the resurrection of Europe, we cannot endure the extreme infamy of witches and heretics literally burned alive—well, the people in this affair were quite as literally burned alive. If, when we have really tried to extend our charity beyond the borders of personal sympathy, to all the complexities of class and creed, we still feel something insolent about the triumphant and acquitted man who is in the wrong, here the men who are in the wrong are triumphant and acquitted. It is no subject for science. It is a subject for poetry. But for poetry of a terrible sort.

www.ingramcontent.com/pod-product-compliance
Lightning Source LLC
Chambersburg PA
CBHW031259130726
47988CB00007B/2647